EVERY STUDENT,
EVERY DAY

A **NO-NONSENSE NURTURER®**
APPROACH TO REACHING ALL LEARNERS

KRISTYN KLEI BORRERO

FOREWORD BY LEE CANTER

Solution Tree | Press
a division of
Solution Tree

555 North Morton Street
Bloomington, IN 47404
800.733.6786 (toll free) / 812.336.7700
FAX: 812.336.7790

email: info@SolutionTree.com
SolutionTree.com

Visit **go.SolutionTree.com/behavior** to download the free reproducibles in this book.

Printed in the United States of America

Library of Congress Cataloging-in-Publication Data

Names: Klei Borrero Kristyn, author.
Title: Every student, every day : a No-Nonsense Nurturer® approach to
   reaching all learners/ Kristyn Klei Borrero.
Description: Bloomington, Indiana : Solution Tree Press, [2018] | Includes
   bibliographical references and index.
Identifiers: LCCN 2018020578 | ISBN 9781947604292 (perfect bound)
Subjects: LCSH: Classroom management.
Classification: LCC LB3013 .K59 2018 | DDC 371.102/4--dc23
LC record available at https://lccn.loc.gov/2018020578

Solution Tree
Jeffrey C. Jones, CEO
Edmund M. Ackerman, President

Solution Tree Press
President and Publisher: Douglas M. Rife
Editorial Director: Sarah Payne-Mills
Art Director: Rian Anderson
Managing Production Editor: Kendra Slayton
Senior Production Editor: Christine Hood
Senior Editor: Amy Rubenstein
Copy Editor: Evie Madsen
Proofreader: Jessi Finn
Editorial Assistant: Sarah Ludwig

ACKNOWLEDGMENTS

To the incredible (past and present) team with whom I work at CT3. You inspire and push me every day. Words can't express the gratitude I experience and the pride I feel in the work we do to impact educators and youth every day.

Special thanks to Noah Borrero for his support and mentorship as I wrote this manuscript and to Karen Klei Schlosser for her ideas and inspiration for the cover design of this book.

Solution Tree Press would like to thank the following reviewers:

Daniel Allen
Principal
Sullivan Elementary School
Sullivan, Illinois

Dan Westfahl
Principal
Brookfield Elementary School
Brookfield, Wisconsin

Randy King
Assistant Principal
Sam Houston Middle School
Garland, Texas

Karen Whetsell
Principal
Suncoast Community High School
Riviera Beach, Florida

Visit **go.SolutionTree.com/behavior** to
download the free reproducibles in this book.

TABLE OF CONTENTS

Reproducible pages are in italics.

PART 1

CHAPTER 4

Use Positive Narration 87

CHAPTER 5

Implement Accountability Systems 105

ABOUT THE AUTHOR

Kristyn Klei Borrero, EdD, is an accomplished educational leader and coach who strives to make a profound difference in the professional lives of educators. Kristyn has committed to improving the education of students in traditionally disenfranchised schools, as a classroom teacher, principal, area superintendent, and cofounder and CEO of the CT3.

Prior to her work with CT3, Kristyn led the research and development of No-Nonsense Nurturer® and Real Time Teacher Coaching®, widely recognized as two of the most innovative, transformative professional development programs in education. She is also a noted contributor to national education blogs, trade journals, and news media.

As an education leader, Kristyn spent 1996–2007 spearheading turnaround initiatives for underperforming schools in Oakland and East Palo Alto, California. She propelled schools under her supervision to significantly exceed all state academic benchmarks, organizational fundraising and financial goals, teacher retention rates, and family and student satisfaction ratings.

Kristyn holds a doctorate in education leadership from the University of California, Berkeley.

To learn more about Kristyn's work, visit www.ct3education.com.

To book Kristyn Klei Borrero for professional development, contact pd@ SolutionTree.com.

FOREWORD

By Lee Canter

I am proud of the work I did with Assertive Discipline®, a model that school leadership teams use to establish a schoolwide behavior management program that supports teachers' classroom efforts. I am grateful for the many teachers who embrace that work and strive to create classrooms where students achieve. However, I know now that my work with Assertive Discipline is incomplete. This work was necessary to our field, but like everything, the next generation of work builds on the effective practices of what came before and, through innovation, often proves even better.

My opportunity to innovate and work on the No-Nonsense Nurturer® model began in 2007 when I met Kristyn Klei Borrero. I was working with a network of urban schools in the Bay Area of California, which were deeply committed to the achievement of traditionally disenfranchised students. Kristyn was one of the eager principals in Oakland, California, I met; at the time, she was completing her doctoral coursework at the University of California, Berkeley. She understood urban youth and critiqued the efficacy of Assertive Discipline in a way that no one else had brought to my attention.

At the insistence of a mutual good friend and colleague, the two of us collaborated to dig deeper and discover what was missing from my previous classroom management work. Together, we found that the biggest pieces missing lived in the area of what we call *life-altering relationships*, specifically how teachers and students communicate with one another and how they work together in the classroom to create authentic engagement.

The No-Nonsense Nurturer® model is the result of our collaboration and subsequent research, having observed hundreds of classrooms and engaged in interviews with endless educators, family members, and students (Klei Borrero & Canter, 2018). This book, *Every Student, Every Day*, is Kristyn's review of what the highest-achieving teachers use to set up classrooms for success, rigor, and caring in culturally relevant ways. This body of work serves students in urban, rural, and suburban schools.

I am proud of cofounding CT3, and since I retired, I am proud of how the work has grown. I am also proud of the countless educators this work has supported and will continue to support. Confidently, I can say that I leave you in great hands. I hope you learn as much as I did on my journey with CT3 and the work of No-Nonsense Nurturers. You deserve the best professional development—and your students deserve the best from you.

The Need for No-Nonsense Nurturers

Necessity is the mother of invention.

—Plato

In my travels as an educational consultant and executive coach, I am constantly reminded of a reality that all too many educators face. While many are well prepared in curriculum, most are not prepared to handle classroom management or support the academic culture necessary for all students to succeed. Teachers spend years studying at universities to learn how to effectively prepare lessons and reach students through content. Yet all that time and expense is potentially meaningless if students don't see your classroom as a culture of high expectations deeply embedded with a relentless belief in what is possible for them.

Because teachers aren't typically well trained in how to develop and maintain a classroom culture that balances strong management with high expectations and relationships, I can only imagine how first-year teachers will feel in their fifth, sixth, seventh, or even twentieth year of teaching. Many teachers will still be struggling with the same issues—disruptive behavior, low engagement, and test scores that don't represent their relentless efforts. *Frustrated* probably doesn't begin to describe their state of mind. This book presents the strategies, concepts, and philosophies of high-performing teachers, each a No-Nonsense Nurturer, and the lessons, mindsets, and strategies we all should have been taught in our teacher preparation programs. Here, in the introduction, I investigate the need and reason for No-Nonsense Nurturers.

The Problem

Since the late 1980s, the education community—educators, reporters, parents, communities, and politicians—have documented the supposed failure of U.S. public schools.

Especially in urban contexts, they place much of the blame directly on teachers and students' families. I believe that this blame is misplaced, and a vital cause stakeholders often overlook or discount is the acute lack of classroom management training the majority of teachers receive (Aloe, Amo, & Shanahan, 2014; Chang, 2009; Marzano, 2003). Because teacher preparation programs have not addressed this need effectively, it is one of the major reasons our profession loses so many educators with unending potential. Therefore, effective classroom management is one of the central themes of this book.

Throughout the book, the terms *classroom management* and *classroom culture* are interchangeable because they are related, but it is important to define and think about them to support your understanding as you read. *Classroom management* refers to the strategies and structures teachers use to keep an orderly, high-functioning environment where students can engage in on-task behaviors that lead to rigorous learning objectives. Classroom management is in service of classroom culture. *Classroom culture* involves the established values, beliefs, and rituals of a classroom that enable strong relationships and high expectations among teacher and students so teaching and learning thrive. With a strong classroom culture, adults and youth are all teachers and learners who share the knowledge, roles, and responsibilities in the classroom environment.

Research validates the importance of teachers' need for effective classroom management training. A major study from the Bill & Melinda Gates Foundation (2010) finds the key to raising students' academic performance is a teacher's ability to establish a positive, disruption-free classroom culture with effective classroom management that promotes student learning.

Other research validates the conclusions of the Bill & Melinda Gates Foundation (2010) study.

▸ Eighty-five percent of new teachers are particularly unprepared or underprepared for dealing with behavior problems in their classroom (Aloe et al., 2014; Hudson, 2012; Public Agenda, 2004).

▸ In many classrooms, teachers spend half of their class time trying to deal with disruptive behavior (Chang, 2009; Cotton & Wikelund 1990; Dicke et al., 2014; Hudson, 2012; Walker, Colvin, & Ramsey, 1995). This is time they could spend on teaching and working on critical-thinking skills.

A report from the National Council on Teacher Quality on teacher training programs summarizes the reality all too many teachers face: "New teachers deserve better. It is time for teacher prep programs to focus on classroom management so that first-year teachers are prepared on day one to head off potential disruption *before* it starts" (Greenberg, Putman, & Walsh, 2014, p. i).

If research identifies the lack of classroom management training as a problem, why don't teacher preparation programs tackle it in order to better prepare and equip future educators? While I have struggled to find research on this, I would hypothesize that classroom management is more difficult to address than other education domains. Why? Because to manage classrooms well, teacher educators and universities would need to evaluate and confront the middle-class cultural norms that are interwoven into the fabric of U.S. school systems (Nieto, 2002; Rist, 1970).

The structural inequities in schools and throughout the history of U.S. public education created norms about behavior and expectations that prioritize white, middle-class values. These cultural norms, which no longer represent most of the students we serve, are particularly evident in classroom management because the discipline in schools is highly cultural—subject to a person's race, gender, and socioeconomic upbringing (Deschenes, Cuban, & Tyack, 2001). Taking on these historical inequities in public education systems would require a deep analysis of culture and race, something that may be uncomfortable, yet necessary for all educators to evaluate.

The Impact

Research indicates the issues that result from ineffective classroom management training have a profoundly negative impact on both teachers and their students.

▸ More than 54 percent of teachers in schools feel discipline problems hinder their ability to teach their students (Aloe et al., 2014; Hudson, 2012; Public Agenda, 2004).

▸ More than 40 percent of teachers quit or are fired from schools within five years, the major reason being their inability to deal with student behavior (Aloe et al., 2014; Chang, 2009; Public Agenda, 2004; Siwatu, 2011).

▸ Students in urban schools have more new, untrained teachers, resulting in lower academic performance than their higher-socioeconomic peers (Emdin, 2016; Marzano, 2003; Peske & Haycock, 2006; Siwatu, 2011).

▶ Students report a sense of alienation from school, believing that no one cares about them (Delpit, 2006; Jensen, 2009; Libbey, 2004; Mouton, Hawkins, McPherson, & Copley, 1996).

Noting this lack of classroom management training and its impact are important for two reasons. First, teacher preparation programs need to better prepare future teachers' abilities to manage classrooms and build strong cultures. It is imperative for all teachers to receive training to effectively establish environments that serve all students from their first day. It is my hope that this book provides a start to this solution, leading teachers and schools to create classroom cultures conducive to student achievement.

Second, if you are reading this book and struggling with classroom management and culture, it is not your fault! You likely never received the proper training or feedback to support the wide variety of student needs and personalities in your classroom. However, it is your professional responsibility to improve your practice as an educator. Reading this book, working through the activities, and reflecting on your current practice support this professional obligation.

I also suggest administrators consider using this book strategically with the professional learning community (PLC) model and as professional development in an effort to align a coherent vision for classroom culture, establish a common language, and set a schoolwide approach to support staff and students. Immense growth occurs in schools when staff work collectively toward practices that embody empowered mindsets and efficacy (Hattie, 2016).

Mindsets refers to the beliefs that affect educators' attitudes and how they view, interpret, and respond to interactions with students and their families. Teachers' cultural beliefs influence their mindsets and impact their points of view, values, and assumptions. Mindsets influence decision making and can empower or disempower relationships with students. However, when teachers understand and reflect on their own mindsets, they can transform them to help build stronger relationships and increase student achievement (Dweck, 2007).

The reality is, the overwhelming majority of teachers, particularly those teaching in traditionally disenfranchised communities or diverse communities, unknowingly harbor disempowering mindsets about the abilities and cultural experiences of their students (Hudson, 2012; Marzano, 2010; Siwatu, 2011). While this may be unintentional, harm to students is immeasurable, as it reflects the larger deficit narrative that much of the education system harbors. Often, this deficit orientation is magnified when teachers haven't had opportunities to reflect on how their mindsets may be impacting their actions. Mindsets impact classroom management more than any other part of education. Why? Because as we manage our classrooms and work to establish cultures for academic success, we bring in our own cultural norms that may or may not match those of our students (Aloe et al., 2014; Hammond, 2015).

Approximately 82 percent of teachers in U.S. public education are of European descent, while only 50 percent of students share a similar background (U.S. Department of Education, 2016). Students in U.S. classrooms are far more diverse than their teachers, and this can be cause for miscommunications and misinterpretations when it comes to classroom expectations. Understanding the cultural and socioeconomic similarities and differences teachers share with students can significantly improve our abilities to support, build relationships with, and teach our students. The authentic relationships we build with students empower our mindsets because they teach us about what is important to students in their communities and in their homes. It is only when we build authentic, deep relationships and learn about students' cultural experiences that we can provide highly engaging, student-focused classrooms.

Overcoming disempowering mindsets, therefore, is essential to teach all students. The good news is that research and experience highlight the most effective way to dismantle disempowering mindsets—by building relationships with students. Students can teach us about their cultures. They can teach us what we need to know about them. Relationships are going to form in your classroom, one way or another, and they need to benefit both you and your students!

Even when educators do not share the same cultural or socioeconomic background as their students, they can still be very effective. While some teachers we studied shared backgrounds with their students, the majority did not (Klei Borrero & Canter, 2018). In short, regardless of your culture and background, you can become a No-Nonsense Nurturer and support the needs of every student, every day. It requires a deep desire to unlearn some of your assumptions about students with humility and through self-reflection about your own learning and teaching, and passion for building meaningful relationships.

The Need for No-Nonsense Nurturers

As a young administrator, I failed to adequately support teachers in my school with classroom management. This was a harsh but true reality of my early administrative years. However, my failures were not for a lack of trying. I bought every book I could find, watched any video I could get my hands on, and sent teachers to seminars and professional development sessions that promised to help them improve classroom management. None of these books, videos, or seminars, however, seemed to answer the one question we needed answered: Why can some teachers establish a classroom culture where students are on task, engaged, and achieving at high academic levels, while their peers struggle?

This question is actually quite complex. In pursuit of an answer, I collaborated with a well-esteemed colleague, Lee Canter. Together, we studied educators across the United States. During these studies:

▸ We observed and interviewed highly effective teachers about their practices.

▸ We interviewed administrators to cross-reference the evidence of these teachers' highly effective classroom practices.

▸ We interviewed students' families about what set apart these high-performing teachers from their peers.

▸ Perhaps most important, we interviewed the students themselves to identify what made these educators stand apart from their other teachers.

A consistent finding across our research indicates that these educators create caring environments for students through consistency, accountability, and high expectations (Klei Borrero & Canter, 2018). These educators establish effective classroom cultures by creating orderly, predictable environments so all students can meet their full potential.

Theoretical Foundations for the No-Nonsense Nurturer Model

It is important to note that the No-Nonsense Nurturer model is grounded in sound education theory. While I consider myself more of a practitioner than an academic, my coursework and my continued work with youth, families, teachers, and administrators has taught me the importance of grounding educational practice in contemporary learning theory. When it comes to applying classroom management models and systems—which can be reactive and rigid—theory must guide our practice. Educators have learned this from decades of research about the most effective ways to promote meaningful learning and teaching in the classroom.

Key research regarding meaningful learning and teaching in the classroom, which was influential in the work of the No-Nonsense Nurturer model, is Sonia Nieto (2002) and her writings about the application of sociocultural theory (Vygotsky 1978).

Foremost in sociocultural theory is the tenet that *learning is social*—it happens through relationships, and the context in which it occurs is vital. Thus, for our purposes as teachers, the classroom culture matters. In her work, Nieto (2002, 2008) applies foundations of sociocultural theory to diverse classrooms and shows that effective learning is rooted in the interrelated concepts of agency, experience, identity, context, and community.

Sociocultural theory stresses that students learn in social and culturally embedded contexts. The concept of *agency* dispels old myths that students are empty vessels teachers fill, and instead asserts that students learn through mutual discovery and relationships with teachers and their peers (Freire, 1970). Teaching is not the practice of transmitting knowledge but rather working alongside learners as they reflect, theorize, and create (or recreate) new knowledge (Nieto, 2002; Picower, 2012; Stefanakis, 2000; Yosso, 2005).

Experience is the second concept of Nieto's (2002) application of sociocultural theory. In education, we tend to take for granted that experience is necessary for learning. Why? Because we may ignore that our students' experiences can differ greatly from our own. In order to share and understand a student's experience, a teacher must build a relationship with each student. When we learn about and better understand our students' experiences, we can then deliver content and pedagogy that is relevant and worthy of our students' learning time.

Closely tied to a student's experience is a student's *identity* and *context*. Identity is closely tied to culture. Culture is complex, and in schools, we often reduce culture to the foods people eat, the holidays they celebrate, or the customs recognized in mainstream society. While these concepts are important, it is only through the relationships we build with students that we learn about their culture, including ethnicity, history, social class, and ways of being and interacting in the world. When we better understand our students as individuals continually navigating multiple cultural contexts every day, we are better able to see them in and through our education environment systems and better position them for success.

The final concept Nieto (2002) presents is *community*, which is strongly rooted in Vygotsky's (1978) notion that society and culture influence learning and if used in positive ways, schools can support student learning. Nieto (2002) notes that teachers can best express this concept by acting as a bridge for students. Through relationships, teachers can acknowledge students' differences and then bridge these differences with the dominant culture in society.

Sociocultural theory supports the importance of relationships in our classrooms and the effort needed to grow these relationships. As educators, it is imperative that we learn about and exercise our relationships with students to provide the best environment for all students to learn, grow, and further develop who they are as individuals and as part of society. This is the true goal of all No-Nonsense Nurturers.

The No-Nonsense Nurturer

Having established the reason for the model's initial research and the theoretical framework, let me explain the term *No-Nonsense Nurturer*. I respectfully refer to the highly effective teachers Lee and I studied as No-Nonsense Nurturers because of the way students reference their highly effective teachers in our interviews with them (Klei Borrero & Canter, 2018). Speaking with students about their teachers and why they are successful in their classroom, many use phrases like "She doesn't play" in the same breath as "She would never let me fail." And they say, "He wants me to stay after school until my homework is done," while at the same time noting, "He comes to my game to cheer me on. He really cares about me." Students essentially talk about the *no-nonsense* qualities of their teachers—refusing to allow their students to fail—while also noting their *nurturing* sides—identifying specific actions these high-performing teachers take to build life-altering relationships with them.

The No-Nonsense Nurturers Lee and I interviewed and studied all noted the importance of relationships with students as part of their success (Klei Borrero & Canter, 2018). To understand what a life-altering relationship really is, take a moment to think back to your high school graduation. If you are like me, while the valedictorian and superintendent spoke, you took some time to reflect on your K–12 education experiences. As I did this, certain teachers stuck out to me because they had a profound impact on who I am as a learner and shaped who I became as a person. Impacting me both as a learner and as a person made these relationships life altering. Like you, as an educator, I want my students to remember me not only for what I taught them but also for how I supported them as individuals and how I made them feel. In the end, I think we all strive to be No-Nonsense Nurturers.

No-Nonsense Nurturers are educators who understand the importance of purposefully building relationships with each student, setting high expectations for every academic challenge, and holding themselves and their students accountable for success with little room for excuses. These teachers work to create environments in which they teach discipline, develop expectations and routines, and create predictable environments to establish trust, respect, and a positive culture.

But how do they do it?

The Four-Step Model

Studying these high-performing teachers, Lee and I notice that they create effective classroom environments using strategies and the following four actions, which we eventually translated into the No-Nonsense Nurturer four-step model (Klei Borrero & Canter, 2018).

1. Give precise directions so every student knows how to be successful with each activity or academic challenge.

2. Narrate positive behaviors of students who get right to work and make choices in the best interest of their learning and the learning of their peers.

3. Implement accountability systems to encourage strong choices, self-discipline, and incentives for collaboration.

4. Build relationships with students beyond academics and really get to know them as individuals.

By using all of these strategies, the teachers built *life-altering relationships* with their students. By establishing a consistent, predictable, fair, and positive environment with the first three strategies, these teachers were able to earn respect, build trust, and set high expectations for students. By grounding it all in relational actions that helped them get to know their students and their students get to know them, they leveraged that initial trust by taking these relationships to transformational levels.

The Foundation of the Model

While building life-altering relationships is the fourth step of the model, it is truly the cornerstone of everything a No-Nonsense Nurturer does. However, relationships take time to build. A teacher's precise directions (step 1) support students with finding success; positive narration (step 2) creates positive momentum in the classroom; and consistent accountability systems (step 3) support a culture of high expectations and care. These first three steps create a path to build life-altering relationships (step 4) that support a student to engage and take risks in the classroom. The power of the four-step model lies in how all the steps work in concert to enhance relationships between teachers and students (and among students) in unique, deep, and lasting ways. It's through these relationships that transformational teaching has the platform to thrive. Precise directions, positive narration, and accountability systems are supports and necessary stepping stones to reaching the fourth step of building life-altering relationships, but none of the four steps can work without the support of the other three.

The types of relationships No-Nonsense Nurturers have with their students are life altering. Life-altering relationships for both students and teachers provide opportunities to transform one another for the better. They define how we communicate and relate with one another in school and ultimately in society. No-Nonsense Nurturers realize that everyone benefits from the relationships they build with students. Through these kinds of relationships, students gain access to rigorous academic content and find trusted adults in their teachers. Teachers who have built such relationships approach their students with an asset-based mindset, thinking about what they can do to help them grow, succeed, and learn. These teachers understand that building relationships is difficult, with ups and downs. Through self-reflection, they learn to adjust their own perceptions as they grow to better understand their students and their cultures.

The students you serve every day—whether from urban, rural, or suburban areas—are masters of their culture, and they are constantly exploring relationships. Students' cultural mastery supports their learning every day. It is up to you to learn from them and use their cultural experiences as assets in your classroom. The best way to do this is through your relationships with them. Through consistent, caring, and interactive discourse, relationships between teachers and students become life altering.

You also must consider the power and importance of building relationships with students' families. No-Nonsense Nurturers recognize the connection each student has to his or her family—culture, experiences, and care. Part of building a strong relationship with students includes building trust and respect with their caregivers. By communicating your expectations to families and making your approach to student learning and classroom culture transparent, you will likely enlist family members as teammates on this journey—ones who want what is best for their children and who will, when they understand your model, aid you in supporting your students.

This book presents the beliefs, attitudes, and techniques No-Nonsense Nurturers utilize to achieve their unique levels of success. I cannot emphasize strongly enough that our research and experience indicates that motivated teachers can learn and master these strategies, beliefs, and attitudes (Klei Borrero & Canter, 2018). You can do this! While it does take a commitment and a growth mindset, this book will support you in making a difference in the lives of every student, every day.

How to Use This Book

If you are reading this book, you will likely do so through one of three lenses—(1) new or struggling teachers, (2) midcareer teachers, or (3) mentor teachers and administrators. However, I hope this book has something to offer *all* educators, no matter where you are in your career.

New or Struggling Teachers

If you are a new or struggling teacher, it is important for you to know you are not alone—we have all been there! All teachers have felt ill-prepared to teach students, struggled to establish a culture of learning, or felt like no matter what they do, students just won't listen or interact with the material. Teaching is the most important and sometimes the most stressful job if you don't have the proper strategies, trainings, and mindsets. I encourage you to read this book with intention and planning. No-Nonsense Nurturer strategies allow you to bring your personality into the classroom and how you choose to implement each strategy through the relationships you build with students. There is no reason you should have to figure it out on your own. This is the playbook of how highly successful educators set the tone for success in their high-performing classrooms.

Midcareer Teachers

Midcareer teachers will likely view this book as a reboot or boost to their current teaching practice. If you are a midcareer teacher who is finding success in your classroom, consider these strategies as affirmation of your practice. Other strategies might be new to you. Take them on! They will support you on your journey as a No-Nonsense Nurturer.

Mentor Teachers and Administrators

As a mentor teacher or administrator, you have an important responsibility to support and coach teachers in your school. Being a successful classroom teacher is an accomplishment; however, finding the language to explain success and coach it effectively is a completely different skill set.

As you read this book, you will find that you already implement some (if not most) of these strategies in your classroom or observe high-performing teachers implementing them in theirs. This book will help you identify and build the language of successful teaching practices you can use to support and coach your teachers to become No-Nonsense Nurturers.

About This Book

This book is divided into two parts. Part 1 investigates the relationship-building paradigms of ineffective and effective educators. This helps set the stage for part 2, which explores the strategies and philosophies of high-performing educators—No-Nonsense Nurturers.

In part 1, chapters 1 and 2 review the relationship-building paradigms many teachers have with their students and how these relationships distract or support classroom management and culture. In part 2, chapters 3 through 6 present the strategies of No-Nonsense Nurturers and the importance relationships play in creating a culture of excellence in highly effective classrooms.

In addition, the end of each chapter provides reproducible reflection activities to support your learning. The reflection activities offer you the opportunity to reflect on your current and future practices and philosophies as No-Nonsense Nurturers. You may complete these reflection activities individually or in collaborative teams. Videos in chapters 3 through 6 offer real-life examples of how teachers use the No-Nonsense Nurturer four-step model in their classrooms.

An Important Note to Readers

I am an urban educator, and I completed the initial research for this book in historically marginalized and traditionally disenfranchised communities (Klei Borrero & Canter, 2018). The original No-Nonsense Nurturers I studied are also urban educators dedicated to combatting the deficit-based narratives about working-class communities of color and their academic achievement in the United States. However, after years of implementing this work in traditionally disenfranchised communities, it is clear that the work of No-Nonsense Nurturers is effective and beneficial for *all* students and teachers. An equitable education system gives all students opportunities to build meaningful relationships with their teachers. It is my hope that this work will support teachers and students in all communities, beyond the urban and rural settings we originally studied. Thank you for trusting me on your journey to become the educator you are meant to be.

Reflection Activities

The reflection activities on pages 13–16 are designed to help you reflect on your current professional practice and support your journey to becoming a No-Nonsense Nurturer. You may choose to complete them individually or in teams.

Preassess Your Relationship With Students

The following questions will help you preassess your current relationship-building paradigms. Read each sentence stem, silently reflect for ten to fifteen seconds, and finish it as honestly as you can. Consider coming back to these sentence stems at the end of chapter 2 after reviewing the relationship-building paradigms—unintended enablers, negative controllers, and No-Nonsense Nurturers.

When it comes to homework, I feel . . .

When students talk about me to their friends, they likely say . . .

When it comes to giving consequences (holding my students accountable) for disruptive behaviors, . . .

If a student enters my classroom clearly tired and puts his or her head down, I am most likely to . . .

If I observe two students pushing each other, I am most likely to say . . .

After assigning a task, I overhear a student a few feet away from me say under his or her breath, "I'm not doing this." I respond by . . .

Track Your Progress Toward Becoming a No-Nonsense Nurturer

One of the ways you'll track your progress to becoming a No-Nonsense Nurturer is to periodically answer the questions and plot your answers on the following continuums. You will return to these continuums after reading chapters 2 and 6.

Place an X on each continuum in the following chart to show where you are today. Use a different-color pen each time you come back to this activity and record the date. Note the evidence (for example, classroom actions, how you think about your relationships with students, and so on) for why you answered the questions the way you did. If you struggle to provide evidence, it is likely you are weaker in this area. Decide on a way to track your progress to ensure your move along the continuum.

Next, place a star at the spot on each continuum to represent where you would like to be by the end of this book—a reasonable and achievable goal.

---

1. How would you characterize your relationships with most of your students?

_____

Weak   Strong

Evidence:

2. About how much time each week do you spend building relationships with students and their families outside of class (this can include before school, planning times during school, after school, or on weekends)?

_____

< Fifteen minutes	One hour	Two hours	Three hours	Four hours	Five hours	> Six hours

Evidence:

3. About what percentage of students are you able to motivate to follow simple directions the first time you state them, without raising your voice?

_____

< 20 percent	40 percent	60 percent	80 percent	85 percent	90 percent	95 percent	100 percent

---

Evidence:

4. What percentage of students are you able to motivate to complete and return homework assignments on time?

< 20 percent	40 percent	60 percent	80 percent	85 percent	90 percent	95 percent	100 percent

Evidence:

5. What percentage, on average, of your students are meeting or exceeding the standards or objectives you teach each day?

< 20 percent	40 percent	60 percent	80 percent	85 percent	90 percent	95 percent	100 percent

Evidence:

6. Approximately what percentage of your students do you find challenging to motivate?

100 percent	85 percent	70 percent	55 percent	40 percent	25 percent	10 percent	0 percent

Evidence:

7. How frequently do you find yourself frustrated with student behavior in your classroom?

Several times a day	Once or twice a day	Once a week	Rarely

Evidence:

Establish Learning Goals

Based on the concepts presented so far, identify two or three learning goals for this book and write them in the chart below.

	My personal learning goal is:	This goal is important to me because:
1		
2		
3		

What one or two steps will you take throughout the book to ensure that you can achieve your goals?	
1	
2	

PART 1

Examining Relationship-Building Paradigms of Effective and Ineffective Classroom Managers

CHAPTER 1

Ineffective Classroom Management: Unintended Enablers and Negative Controllers

G iven the amount of time teachers and students spend together over the course of a year, relationships will form and evolve. It is inevitable. How productive these relationships are for both teachers and students, however, is left to question.

This chapter examines two ineffective relationship-building paradigms teachers tend to develop because they may lack training, support, or self-awareness—(1) unintended enablers, teachers who lead with their feelings and are often uncomfortable taking a firm stand in their classrooms, thereby unintentionally allowing students to be off task; and (2) negative controllers, teachers who tend to be overly strict, unpredictable, and often put their needs before their students' in order to keep controlled, disruption-free classrooms. Teachers who embrace these paradigms struggle with classroom management and classroom culture. This chapter will help educators recognize any tendencies in their own practices and support them to diminish or hopefully eliminate them.

The paradigms of unintended enablers and negative controllers are sweeping generalizations and are not prescriptive, nor are they completely comprehensive descriptions. In fact, the descriptions on the following pages are extreme examples of these types of relationship-building paradigms. At best, the practices of unintended enablers and negative controllers can work in supporting the achievement of some students in their classrooms. At worst, however, these two relationship paradigms can have detrimental, sometimes damaging and devaluing repercussions for teacher-student relationships and achievement.

You may discover that some of your relationship-building strategies align with those of unintended enablers, while others align more with negative controllers. You may also find that you already build relationships using strategies that resemble those of No-Nonsense Nurturers, the third paradigm (see chapter 2, page 35). Understanding all three relationship-building paradigms (unintended enablers, negative controllers, and No-Nonsense Nurturers) will help you become more aware of your developing relationships and classroom culture. Be reflective as you read about the attributes, motivations, impact, and mindsets of these relationship-building paradigms throughout this book, but don't be hard on yourself if you find some unintended enabling or negative controlling tendencies resonating with you. Bring your humility to the table, set new goals, and decide on some new ways to build relationships with students.

The following sections review some of the common attributes, motivations, and mindsets of unintended enablers and negative controllers, including possible outcomes for students as a result of interacting with teachers with these characteristics.

Unintended Enablers

Some teachers lead with their hearts. Those who lead with their feelings, making excuses for students, are often uncomfortable taking a firm stand in their classrooms or holding students accountable for their learning, thereby unintentionally allowing students to be off task and disconnect from learning opportunities—these are the *unintended enablers*.

Teachers with these tendencies *unintentionally enable* their students. They keep students from reaching or exceeding their potential by lowering expectations because they feel sorry for them, feel bad about the circumstances in which they live, or fear the repercussions of holding them accountable. While a sense of empathy for students is necessary for all teachers, unintended enablers often amass a series of excuses for why students cannot rise to high academic standards. These lowered expectations and excuses quickly catch up to students and ultimately harm their ability to succeed in school and in society.

> Early in my career, I shared many of my middle school students with Ms. Emerling. Ms. Emerling was a bit older than me, skilled in her craft in many ways, but distracted by the complications some of our students faced. Her skillful teaching was often replaced by engaging with a single student in need of support instead of engaging with all students. In short, she often lowered her standards for the students we shared because she felt sorry for them.

To be fair, Ms. Emerling had an amazing heart and work ethic. She worked tirelessly to make sure her students had the clothes they needed, food in their bellies, and field trips to new places. She spent much of her free time fundraising and collecting recycled clothes and school supplies, but often to the detriment of her lesson-planning time.

While she worked to build relationships with each of her students, most walked out of her middle school classroom ill-prepared for the next stage of their education careers, not because she wasn't a great teacher but because she focused on students' circumstances rather than their abilities and capabilities. I truly admired her heart (and her stamina), but her lowered expectations in the end did not set up students for success. Ms. Emerling was a true unintended enabler.

Unintended enablers often have their hearts in the right place, but their actions, unfortunately, are counterproductive. Several disempowering mindsets that may cause unintended outcomes motivate these teachers' behaviors. The disempowered mindsets of unintended enablers usually stem from their fear of student reactions or feeling sorry or making excuses for their students. Examining some of the common mindsets of unintended enablers will support you in building stronger relationships with students and likely provide you with greater satisfaction in your classroom.

"I Don't Want to Be Mean or Strict"

A common attribute of unintended enablers is that they tend to be reluctant to take charge of their classroom because they don't want to be "mean" to students. Rather than clearly communicating expectations to students, such as saying, "There is no talking at this time," and, if appropriate, providing a consequence, unintended enablers may do or say one of the following.

- Make weak (sometimes pleading) ineffectual disciplinary statements.
  - "Please listen to me."
  - "Come on, I can't teach if you're talking."
- Threaten discipline, but then not follow through.
  - "I'm tired of you constantly talking when I'm trying to teach. I will give you detention, so don't keep testing me."
  - "Next time you talk back, I'm calling your mom. I mean it this time."

▸ Enter into negotiations with students in the hopes their behaviors will change.

  ▷ "If you calm down and stop crying, I won't call your grandmother."

  ▷ "If you stop giving me attitude and get back to work, I'll give you another chance and you won't have to serve detention."

▸ Ask questions or seek permission from students.

  ▷ "Will you please take your seat? I really need to move forward with the lesson."

  ▷ "Ladies, can you finish your conversation? We need to move to the hallway, and we don't want to interrupt other classes."

The fear of being mean or strict often arises from communication differences between teachers and students because of socioeconomic, cultural, or racial background differences. When some students hear the teacher's tone (negotiating, seeking permission, and so on), they think they have a choice, while the teacher thinks he or she has communicated an expectation. This miscommunication between the teacher and students is unintentional, but if given a choice, students may not meet the intended expectation, causing frustration for the teacher and sometimes unwarranted consequences for students.

The work of educator and author Lisa D. Delpit (2006) helps clarify this issue. She postulates that, in general, most educators raised in middle-class homes had parents or guardians who spoke to them in an indirect manner. She identifies this indirect approach as more democratic in nature, as adults may allow children to express their opinions, ask questions, or negotiate rules and expectations.

For example, if an indirect parent wants his or her child to get ready for dinner, he or she might say the following.

Parent (question): "I think it's time to put away your toys?"

Child: "Hmmm . . ."

Parent (statement of opinion): "I think it's time to put away your game and wash up for dinner."

Child: "But I'm in the middle of a game."

Parent (negotiation): "Then how about finishing the game and then washing up?"

Even though the parent's words are *indirect*—that is, couched as a question, a statement of opinion, and a negotiation—both the adult and child understand it is a *directive* to put away the game and get ready for dinner.

In contrast, some parents or guardians communicate with their children in a more *authoritarian* manner, which may be an unfamiliar practice for some teachers (Bradley, Corwyn, Burchinal, McAdoo, & Coll, 2001; Brooks-Gunn & Markman, 2005; Jensen, 2009). These parents or guardians often speak to their children in a direct, firm, and some might say, *demanding* manner (Delpit, 2006; Ladd & Fiske, 2011).

For example, if an authoritarian or direct parent wants his or her child to put away toys and get ready for dinner, he or she might say the following.

> **Parent (demand):** "It's time for dinner. You need put away the video game and any other toys that are out."

If the child tries to negotiate or argue, the response is typically direct.

> **Child:** "But I'm in the middle of a game."
>
> **Parent:** "Don't argue with me . . . put away the toys and get ready for dinner."

Thus, a child being raised by a more authoritarian parent or guardian typically learns that if a loving adult expects the child to listen to directions, he or she does not ask questions, state opinions, or negotiate. Rather, the authoritarian parent or guardian gives a directive, often in a firm tone of voice, stating what he or she wants done. If a teacher takes an indirect approach with children who are used to a more authoritarian approach, they may interpret the request as optional, when the teacher believes he or she stated it as an expectation. This type of cultural misunderstanding, often aligned with race or socioeconomic status, can lead to misaligned expectations resulting in behavior challenges and broken relationships. However, because the teacher is in the power position, he or she often blames the student for the lack of understanding, leading to unexamined or unnecessary behavioral challenges.

What is the possible outcome of this disempowering mindset in the classroom? If teachers do not create clear communications and positive relationships, then the classroom culture may be void of consistent expectations. Disruptive behaviors can become the norm and opportunities for academic achievement can go unfulfilled. These teachers' inability to influence students' academic achievement or social development can result in teachers being frustrated and leaving the profession (Aloe et al., 2014; Berry, Hopkins-Thompson, & Hoke, 2002; Chang, 2009; Freedman & Appleman, 2009; Haberman, 2004b), and students missing academic opportunities.

"I Can't Get My Students to Behave Because My Administrator Doesn't Support Discipline"

Many unintended enablers struggle with holding their students accountable, so instead they try to rely on school leadership. If the school leader falls short of teacher expectations, this can quickly become a reason why an unintended enabler struggles to support students through their difficult days and gives up on students engaging in academic work (Kafele, 2013).

What is the possible outcome of this disempowering mindset in the classroom? Like teachers, administrators often become overwhelmed (Farkas, Johnson, Duffett, & Foleno, 2001). If teachers and administrators do not work together to support student behaviors and outcomes, some students will fall through the net of the education system, experiencing low grades, inappropriate placement in special education, dropping out of school, or even incarceration. As a result, as adults, these youths will likely need additional supports or assistance.

"I Get Nervous About Students' Reactions When I Try to Hold Them Accountable"

Unintended enablers may shy away from holding certain students accountable for their work and actions because the teachers are afraid of the students' reactions— physically or emotionally (Klei Borrero & Canter, 2018). Furthermore, these teachers haven't learned the strategies to support a student who might talk back, argue, or become defiant. Their fear of a student's reaction to being held accountable becomes an excuse and a reason unintended enablers give up on certain students and don't hold them accountable—they give up in order to keep peace in the classroom.

Some common attributes or relationship-building strategies of unintended enablers include the following.

- ▶ Ignoring inappropriate student behaviors or comments
- ▶ Overly praising students for the smallest accomplishments, thus lowering overall expectations
- ▶ Sharing too much personal information with students in an attempt to become friends with them
- ▶ Trying to be "cool" by pretending to share students' tastes in music, video games, or other interests

What is the possible outcome of this disempowering mindset in the classroom? These attributes corrupt the students' ability to achieve and the teachers' ability to make a difference in their lives (Duncan-Andrade, 2007; Steele, 2004). The cool or friend persona often accounts for mediocre expectations and aligned outcomes. Students don't tend to respect teachers they see as their peers; this can be quite challenging when a mentoring relationship of mutual respect is necessary between teacher and student. Without a respectful relationship, classrooms can become volatile and learning doesn't reach its full potential.

"I Can't Expect Students With So Many Challenges to Achieve"

Many teachers fall victim to the "soft bigotry of low expectations" ("Excerpts from Bush's speech," 1999). They believe their students face so many challenges, such as poverty, neglect, parental demands, or societal pressures, that lowering their demands on students seems fair and compassionate (Farr, 2010).

Unintended enablers often make excuses for their students because they feel sorry for them. The challenges these students encounter—poverty, bullying, and pressures experienced with social media, violence, unstable households, unattainable demands from family members, illness, and trauma—are real. Do these challenges make it harder for them to be successful at school? Of course they do! But what is the cost of lowering expectations for these students? They miss educational opportunities, thus limiting their choices and opportunities for the rest of their lives (Jussim & Harber, 2005; Rosenthall & Jacobson, 1968; Tenenbaum & Ruck, 2007).

With this disempowered mindset, unintended enablers may hesitate to push students academically because they feel sorry for their circumstances at home or in the community, or for medical reasons, as in the following examples.

> Norman has a really hard life. His grandparents are raising him, and he really misses his mom. How can I expect him to complete all of his homework?
>
> Shayla has always struggled in school. Now that she's in tenth grade, how can I expect her to keep up with the class?
>
> I don't think Jake's parents ever read to him. This first-grade work is developmentally inappropriate for him.
>
> Zach's attention deficit hyperactivity disorder is so severe, I am just happy when he stays in his seat and isn't disruptive to the other students' learning.
>
> Katie's dad is so hard on her. He expects straight As and extra homework. I need to go easier on Katie while she is at school. Otherwise, she will burn out before high school.

What is the possible outcome of this disempowering mindset in the classroom? While this compassion is commendable, and circumstances may be tough for some students, when we lower our expectations, each year students fall further and further behind academically (Milner, 2007). This often has crippling effects on their future academics, especially after a year or two of experiencing teachers with lowered expectations. For some students, after a few years of lowered expectations, they will struggle throughout their academic careers (Jussim & Harber, 2005; Rosenthall & Jacobson, 1968; Tenenbaum & Ruck, 2007). Excuses (instead of solutions) further disempower students and rob them of educational opportunities. Demands on students are real, and if teachers don't help them navigate these demands, they will fall further and further behind in what is necessary to achieve in a 21st century learning environment and job market.

Unintended enablers have their hearts in the right place, but they often compromise their impact. When students are exposed to these types of teachers over time, they will fall further and further behind academically and miss opportunities for achievement. Ultimately, this relationship-building paradigm can lead students to believe that adults hold low expectations for them, which transfers to how they see and perceive themselves throughout school and life (Steele, 2004).

Negative Controllers

While unintended enablers share some qualities with negative controllers, these relationship-building paradigms tend to be quite different; however, both adversely impact students and teachers over time.

As a student (or now as a teacher), you may have had some teachers exhibit negative, controlling attitudes when interacting with you or other students in class. Negative controllers tend to be overly strict and unpredictable in their consequences, and they tend to pick on certain students while letting others slide. Negative controllers also tend to be intolerant of certain student needs or behaviors and struggle to understand the importance of relationships in a learning environment. Their intolerance and lack or absence of relationships may show up as aggressively advocating for zero-tolerance discipline policies that put their needs before those of their students in order to keep controlled, disruption-free classrooms (Duncan-Andrade, 2007).

While teachers with negative controlling attributes often lack fairness, they do want students to succeed and strive to have the quiet classroom their administrators and colleagues admire. The disempowered mindsets of negative controllers denote their need for control and lack of relationships with students because of their negativity.

Examining some of the common mindsets of this relationship-building paradigm will help you examine your own mindsets about the students you serve and support.

"It's Impossible to Expect 100 Percent of Students to Be Engaged 100 Percent of the Time"

Negative controllers often struggle with their relationships with students. Instead of being accountable for those struggles, these teachers often place blame on their students' circumstances, the challenges they face, or the students themselves.

Negative controllers tend to believe in self-motivated students, but if students need or expect extra assistance, teachers often leave them behind for the greater good of the class. You might hear these teachers make statements such as:

- "She has chosen not to do the work; if she fails, it's not my fault."

- "I can't let one kid derail the whole class; he is out of here. The rest of us want to learn."

- "The classroom is like a bell curve; not all students can be challenged, and some may have to be left behind."

Teachers with this relationship-building paradigm are often quick to dismiss students because of needs they might not know how to address (for example, the needs of exceptional or students you find challenging), so the needs of 100 percent of students rarely get met in these classrooms (Noguera, 2003; Valenzuela, 1999).

As a way of managing, negative controllers may overzealously assert their authority in an effort to ensure they control their classrooms. They might speak in a demeaning, sarcastic, or angry tone to compensate for irrelevant lessons or a lack of strategies to build relationships or support students' academic needs. Rather than preparing relevant lessons, meeting students, and clearly communicating, negative controllers often expect students to "just know what to do." This mindset may come across like one of the following.

- Using aggressive, sarcastic statements or body language (such as rolling eyes or a shaking head)
  - "What, are you deaf today?"
  - "I don't get it, Anthony. You seemed smart yesterday."
  - "How many times do I have to tell you?"
  - "Really? You don't get it?" (said under the teacher's breath)

- ▶ Disciplining students too quickly, unfairly, or inconsistently
  - ▷ "I'm tired of you being constantly off topic. Just get out if you don't want to learn."
  - ▷ "I can't deal with you and your attitude today. Go to the dean for the remainder of the period."
  - ▷ "I'm sick of you talking constantly; go sit in the hallway."
- ▶ Not recognizing students who need to be challenged
  - ▷ "I'm not sure why Damian didn't show growth on his assessments. He got As on all the work I provided for him. Guess it was just a bad testing day for him."
  - ▷ "I know certain students aren't being challenged, but I can't get to all thirty of my students in one day. I'm sure they will find something new in this lesson."

What is the possible outcome of this disempowering mindset in the classroom? If students don't feel like their teachers care for them, it is unlikely they will learn. Students often misinterpret sarcasm as statements of truth. Aggressive tones and negative body language can impact their psyche and willingness to engage. If all students are not invited to engage in discussion and experimentation at high levels in the classroom, deep learning will never happen. While negative controllers often think they have high-functioning, quiet classrooms, students often perceive these environments as mean and judgmental where high-quality learning (and instruction) is lacking.

"It Is My Job to Teach; It Is the Students' Job to Learn"

A negative controller may see his or her role as solely teacher of academic content and subject matter (rather than of students). In order to teach students, teachers must have a relationship with them. Negative controllers may forget to humanize their students in a quest to teach content. These teachers often believe if they have spent the time lesson planning and preparing for the day's learning, it is up to students to learn the content, when in fact, as teachers, our responsibility doesn't end with teaching—it includes being accountable for student growth and learning (Kafele, 2013).

Statements by negative controllers might sound like the following.

- ▶ "I prepare my lessons every day. It is up to the students to decide whether or not they want to learn the material. I have no control over that."

▸ "I work hard. I should be able to expect the same from the students. So many of them are so lazy or unmotivated."

▸ "I don't understand why José is failing American history. When I was in school, I loved this topic."

Because negative controllers believe they are in school to teach, they tend to lose patience with poor student behaviors or lack of engagement. This frequently results in inconsistent discipline practices because these teachers don't realize they haven't set clear expectations or given precise directions to students to ensure success (Duncan-Andrade, 2007; Yang, 2009). If a task isn't completed properly, one student's consequence may be a simple reminder, while another student receives more severe consequences (often because of past behaviors or the way the teacher feels about the student). This is often due to lack of teacher training.

What is the possible outcome of this disempowering mindset in the classroom? Teachers have many jobs—teaching content and building relationships are just two of them. But one cannot sacrifice one for the other. Both are necessary to keep a highly engaged, fair, and consist environment for learning. When one is lacking, inconsistent classroom management practices further exacerbate poor relationships with students. In a negative controller's classroom, students may initially stay on task out of fear, but eventually some students may attempt to get back at the teacher through overt or covert classroom disruptions.

In addition, students have a keen sense of social justice. When students feel they or their peers are being treated unfairly, it often shifts their focus to the classroom injustices, distracting them from academic engagement and perpetuating behaviors likely unconducive to an academically challenging environment where all students thrive (Picower, 2012).

"I Have So Much Curriculum to Get Through; I Don't Have Time to Ensure Everyone Is With Me All the Time"

The amount of curriculum and content teachers must cover can overwhelm any teacher but especially those with negative controller tendencies. Because of their need to be successful, relationships often get overlooked, content is moved through quickly, and as time passes, more students are left struggling because of their unmet needs.

Statements from a negative controller might sound like the following.

▸ "It doesn't matter what we do, we have tried everything, and no one is successful with Clive."

▶ "Marquis has a hard life, but so do all the other kids. Being a kid these days is hard. He just needs to bear down and get his work done, or he is going to fail at this game we call life."

▶ "Cecilia has always struggled in school. It is about time she catches up because high school graduation is only a few years away."

▶ "I have taught this already a bunch of times; I can't help it if he isn't learning it."

▶ "I feel sorry for my top students. I never have time to challenge them."

What is the possible outcome of this disempowering mindset in the classroom? While teachers meet curriculum map timelines, it is often at the expense of relationships with students and learning. While students' test scores might be slightly higher than those of their peers with unintended enabling tendencies, their achievement tends to be represented in the lower levels of educational psychologist Benjamin S. Bloom's (1956) taxonomy (knowledge and comprehension) (Pope, 2001). Many students do not feel challenged in a negative controller's classroom.

"Students Should Respect Me Just Because I Am the Teacher"

Many teachers enter the classroom believing they should be granted authority by the nature of their position. On the other hand, many students expect teachers to earn their authority through their words and actions (Obidah & Teel, 2001). Much conflict can arise over authority issues between a teacher who *expects* to receive respect and students who will only give respect if the teacher *earns* it. Consistency, predictability, and follow-through are the best ways to earn students' respect. Negative controllers often overlook the necessity of these qualities and make decisions based on their own needs instead of their students'.

Because negative controllers feel students should respect them, a common attribute of these teachers is to threaten students to get them back on task or when a student gets upset. This attribute often comes from a lack of training on how to handle different types of interactions with students or an inability to build effective relationships with them. These negative controllers might sound like the following.

▶ "Stop giving me attitude and get back to work, or you will be seeing the inside of the detention room for a week."

▶ "You need to calm down. If you can't, I will call your mother right here, right now, and let her know that you don't care about learning."

What is the possible outcome of this disempowering mindset in the classroom? Unfortunately, the teacher's inability to communicate high expectations, respond positively to student needs, and build relationships demonstrates for students that adults in a position of authority are often untrustworthy, and may rob the students of opportunities and access—in school and in society.

The need to control the classroom motivates negative controllers, as their name indicates, often with negative tendencies. These teachers aim to control the student behaviors, volume in the classroom, and content taught. Negative controllers often fear that if they do not remain in control of the classroom, student behaviors will quickly get out of hand and students will not master academic content. Their counterproductive interactions with students often create roadblocks in building strong relationships (Duncan-Andrade, 2007) instrumental for all students and their learning, but especially those growing up in communities with high levels of poverty (Nieto, 2002; Picower, 2012; Valenzuela, 1999).

Conclusion

This chapter discussed the relationship-building paradigms of unintended enablers and negative controllers. You may have recognized certain attributes or behaviors in yourself as you read. Remember, this is not a time for blame or remorse; this type of reflection is an opportunity to learn, grow, and build on your training as an educator. Much of what we do in the classroom is done based on what we think is best for students. Until we learn new ways to shift our thinking and behaviors, our teaching and relationships with students are unlikely to change. Take note of the things you want to work on with your students. The next chapter reviews the more powerful and impactful relationship-building paradigm of No-Nonsense Nurturers.

Reflection Activities

The reflection activities on pages 32–33 are designed to help you reflect on your current professional practice and support your journey to becoming a No-Nonsense Nurturer. You may choose to complete them individually or in teams.

Identify Your Attributes

It is likely you have some attributes of an unintended enabler, a negative controller, or maybe both; most of us do. Take ten minutes to jot down some attributes you would like to work on to avoid your students misinterpreting your intentions. Then take an additional five minutes to note the attributes you want to ensure you keep as a teacher.

Mindsets and Attributes of Unintended Enablers I Would Like to Work On	Mindsets and Attributes of Negative Controllers I Would Like to Work On	Mindsets and Attributes I Want to Ensure I Continue to Use and Nurture

How will you use your assets as a teacher to overcome some of your unintended enabler or negative controller attributes?

Record Your Teaching

Teachers walk into the classrooms every day ready to do their best for each of their students. While teaching a lesson, record yourself for ten to twenty minutes. Review the lesson, taking notes and writing down direct quotes of when you see unintended enabler or negative controller tendencies. Then, go back and rewrite your script.

How might you respond to students differently next time?

What questions could you have asked to support learning?

Is there a sarcastic comment you could avoid next time?

How might you want to restate the directions?

What can you do to ensure the lesson is relatable to students in your classroom?

Did you take advantage of relationship-building opportunities?

CHAPTER 2

Effective Classroom Management: No-Nonsense Nurturers

Now that you have investigated the relationship-building paradigms of unintended enablers and negative controllers, let's take a closer look at how No-Nonsense Nurturers build relationships with their students. The stark difference between ineffective relationship-building paradigms and those of No-Nonsense Nurturers is the relationships these highly effective teachers build with students, the positive tone they set in their classroom, and the high expectations they believe each student can achieve. These elements encompass the words, actions, and strategies they employ in their classrooms—*with every student, every day.*

I was blessed in my first year of teaching. I started my career in Princeton City Schools in Southwest Ohio, and like many districts, the human resources department assigned me a mentor, Patricia Hooks Gray. Ms. Gray was a No-Nonsense Nurturer. Of course at the time, the term didn't exist, but she was an amazing educator and support for me to better my practice. Ms. Gray modeled for and coached me on how to best support my students. She noticed my assets as well as the areas that I needed to improve as a teacher. She consistently used my assets to support my opportunities for growth. For example, I was great at building relationships with my students, but I would sometimes get lazy with lesson planning and begin "shooting from the hip."

Ms. Gray pointed out to me that my relationship with students was the reason they wanted to learn from me and with me; however, she also helped me self-assess the days I was well-planned verses those where I was shooting from the hip. Through simple assessments,

continued →

she quickly helped me realize that my students weren't getting as much from the lessons on the days I was not well planned. She also held me accountable to the fact that because my relationships with students were so strong, I owed them my best every day. Otherwise, I would be taking advantage of the respect I had earned and my positional power as a teacher.

Ms. Gray was a No-Nonsense Nurturer to me. She was my mentor, and I was her student. But she also modeled how to be a great teacher. When I would observe her teaching, students moved through her classroom procedures flawlessly and engaged in deep conversations. She rarely taught students, rather she facilitated their discussions with well-planned questions and curriculum that was relevant to them. She challenged them both academically and in how they saw themselves contributing to their communities and the larger society.

Ms. Gray held high expectations for her students, listening to their excuses but always turning their excuses into opportunities for learning. If a student got a grade on a test or paper that was not satisfactory to her, she gave him or her another chance to retake the test or provided additional support or tutoring so the student could raise his or her grade. Because her students thought so highly of her and spoke about her at home, I would often walk into her classroom to find family members seeking advice about their children. Ms. Gray had a way of giving families advice without ever judging their actions. I learned more from her in my first year of teaching than I did in my entire four years of college as an undergrad.

Through research, I have learned that most No-Nonsense Nurturers weren't born with these motivations, attributes, and mindsets; they listened to their students, observed great teachers, and had mentors who supported their development and mindsets (Klei Borrero & Canter, 2018). Becoming a No-Nonsense Nurturer isn't a destination—it is a journey. With each incoming class of students, new learning takes place because these teachers are relentless in their pursuit of 100 percent student engagement, 100 percent of the time.

Before analyzing the successful strategies of No-Nonsense Nurturers, it is important to review the attributes, motivations, impacts, and mindsets of these highly effective teachers. You will likely already be implementing many of these practices, but be sure to read critically for how you might tweak or even change your practice to better serve students and increase your success in the classroom.

No-Nonsense Nurturer Attributes

What does it take to be a No-Nonsense Nurturer? Following are some of the attributes and characteristics of No-Nonsense Nurturers and the effect they can have on student relationships and learning.

▸ No-Nonsense Nurturers understand that their relationships with students and high expectations drive strong student achievement. These teachers don't accept failure. They meet all students where they are and push them to achieve more than they may realize they are capable of. These teachers incorporate formative assessment and data-driven instructional practices to adjust their lessons for students who might need extra support or enrichment (Fisher & Frey, 2013). They use the relationships and structures they build with students to support student learning, social-emotional development, and confidence by providing a caring, supportive environment where all learners are valued.

▸ No-Nonsense Nurturers not only hold their students to a high standard but also themselves. They use every minute they have with their students, are well prepared for lessons, and organize their time so they can balance a personal life as well as meet students' needs.

▸ No-Nonsense Nurturers never give up on their students. They are relentless in the pursuit of finding what works for every student and assume the best in him or her. They believe each student can exceed expectations and portray this in their words and actions when working with students (Bondy, Ross, Hambacher, & Acosta, 2013; Ladson-Billings, 1994). No-Nonsense Nurturers realize every student is a puzzle, some easier to figure out than others, but when they do, the rewards are beyond any standardized testing measure.

▸ No-Nonsense Nurturers hold students accountable for completing their academic assignments, expect all students to engage in learning, and help students recognize challenges as chances to grow and learn. No-Nonsense Nurturers motivate students to remain engaged in assignments and work to the best of their abilities. If students do not meet the teachers' high expectations, these teachers take the actions needed to support their students so they do not miss learning opportunities (Adkins-Coleman, 2010; Wilson & Corbett, 2001).

▸ No-Nonsense Nurturers use a positive, strong voice and tone (as needed and appropriate) when dealing with student behavior and setting expectations for learning to communicate urgency and importance in the classroom (Lemov, 2015).

▸ No-Nonsense Nurturers have an expanded view and, in many ways, redefine their role as educators. Highly effective teachers do more than merely provide academic content in their classrooms. They also provide the extra support needed to help students succeed in class and in life (Kopp, 2011). Having an expanded view of their role helps No-Nonsense Nurturers develop life-altering relationships with students because they know that for many students, a positive relationship with the teacher is a precondition for meaningful school experiences (Brown, 2004; Jensen, 2009; Milner, 2006; Valenzuela, 1999).

▸ No-Nonsense Nurturers see themselves as important and caring adults in the lives of their students. No-Nonsense Nurturers' students often refer to their teachers as *second parents*, and these teachers take that role seriously, caring for students' emotional health and well-being (Weinstein & Mignano, 2003). Students often note that their teacher is someone they can count on and *has their back*. Even when teachers seem strict or firm in the classroom, students interpret this coming from deep caring. Students understand that accountability and high expectations support them in their future success. They understand their teachers want what is best for them, just as a family member would.

▸ Having a No-Nonsense Nurturer view of teaching requires demonstrating a different kind of caring. Instead of simply being nice to their students by making positive comments to them and interacting with them during the instructional day (Nieto, 2008; Shevalier & McKenzie, 2012; Weinstein, 1998), No-Nonsense Nurturers recognize that demonstrating care to students requires truth, authenticity, and respect.

No-Nonsense Nurturer Motivations

No-Nonsense Nurturers are highly motivated to build relationships with students, realizing the benefits these relationships have on student learning and achievement and on their own professional development and job satisfaction. Following are several of the motivations driving No-Nonsense Nurturers in the classroom.

▸ For No-Nonsense Nurturers, building life-altering relationships with students is fundamental to establishing a classroom culture where motivated students achieve at high levels. Teachers must enter classrooms with a foundational belief in their students' capabilities and a desire to build authentic relationships that honor students' life experiences (Borrero, 2011; Camangian, 2010; Hammond, 2015). This is an important motivation for No-Nonsense Nurturers. These teachers build life-altering relationships with students that also bring satisfaction in their own careers and make them feel they are making a difference in the lives of future generations.

▸ No-Nonsense Nurturers have a burning desire to positively influence students' lives. This desire often arises from an intense sense of social justice and activism, as well as a belief that education is a civil rights issue (Losen & Skiba, 2010; McAllister & Irvine, 2002; Milner, 2006).

▸ Many No-Nonsense Nurturers talk about their work as a matter of life or death for students who are overcoming challenges associated with poverty, violence, and limited opportunities (Klei Borrero & Canter, 2018; National Research Council, 2004). No-Nonsense Nurturers do not operate from a *savior mentality*; rather, they operate from a desire to learn with and from their students. They understand that education provides students with choices for the future. To that end, No-Nonsense Nurturers approach every day of learning with their students as precious and are mindful not to miss learning or relationship-building opportunities.

Many important benefits arise from how No-Nonsense Nurturers interact with their students, including the following.

▸ No-Nonsense Nurturers build life-altering relationships with students, which enable them to academically challenge students beyond what negative, controlling, or enabling teachers can.

▸ No-Nonsense Nurturers establish mutually respectful, academically achieving, equitable classroom cultures that empower students to take risks and learn at high levels (Delpit, 2012; Ross, Bondy, Gallingane, & Hambacher, 2008).

▸ No-Nonsense Nurturers consistently support students to put forth their best efforts, resulting in high academic achievement and confidence (for teachers and students).

▸ No-Nonsense Nurturers have positive, life-altering experiences that result from the relationships they develop with students. Many of these teachers report being better people because of these relationships (Klei Borrero & Canter, 2018). Their students teach these teachers about situations and factors they would not normally consider. Their students help them build a better lens and sense of reality of what is happening in the communities where they teach. No-Nonsense Nurturers recognize any bias they may bring to their teaching and reflect on it to ensure it doesn't impact their ability to effectively reach all students.

▸ No-Nonsense Nurturers enjoy their work as educators and have long, fruitful careers, impacting thousands of students' lives because of the empowered mindsets they have about their students and their own abilities as educators. These teachers report loving their jobs despite the constant demands of standardized testing and the politics among the adults in many schools.

Empowering Mindsets of No-Nonsense Nurturers

The empowering mindsets of No-Nonsense Nurturers center on holding high expectations for 100 percent of their students, 100 percent of the time, and developing positive, life-altering relationships with students and their families. Consider the following.

"I Get Into My Students' Hearing"

When managing the success of twenty-five or more students in a classroom, clear, concise, and often direct communication is important so you can *get into your students' hearing* and they follow your directions. What does *get into your students' hearing* mean? As teachers, we may use language conventions that are confusing to students or miscommunicate our expectations. For example, a teacher might ask, "Students, can you please put away your materials?" when he or she really means, "Students, it is time to put away your materials." The difference in your tone and intonation can determine whether students perceive your words as a question—giving them a choice in the situation— or understand that you are stating an expectation. Getting into your students' hearing means you recognize that there is a difference in your communication style and the communication style your students are used to. Some teachers struggle with getting into their students' hearing because they are afraid that by being direct, they sound mean. However, for many students, using clear, concise, and direct language when setting expectations shows students a confident teacher with expectations everyone must follow and high confidence in each student's ability to be successful.

If teachers are unsuccessful in communicating expectations with students, there is a risk of students misinterpreting what the teachers want. This can result in teachers feeling certain students are noncompliant and, as a result, they may become frustrated. All this could be happening while students think they are following directions, which can lead to consequences for both teachers and students.

Following are two scenarios that illustrate this point.

Scenario One

> **Unintended enabler:** "Students, I think we've spent enough time reading. Let's put away your reading books. Take out your journals and get started on your writing lesson for the day."
>
> **What students might hear:** "The teacher thinks we've spent enough time on our reading, and when we are ready, she would like us to take out our journals."

So, some students feel they can choose what to do. Some students continue reading, while others begin writing, to the consternation of the teacher.

Scenario Two

> **No-Nonsense Nurturer:** "Students, we have spent twenty minutes reading. Silently put away your reading books and take out your journals. We will begin our writing lesson in thirty seconds."
>
> **What students hear:** "The teacher expects me to put my reading book away and take out my journal now."

A firm, clear tone sends a message students understand clearly and, as a result, they are more likely to follow the directions in a timely manner.

When giving directions to students, it is important to get into your students' hearing so they can be successful. It is important to note that the No-Nonsense Nurturer example does not suggest that teachers must always speak in a firm, direct tone. In fact, there are many times during instructional periods when this tone is unnecessary.

No-Nonsense Nurturers understand the difference and adjust between the tone of a no-nonsense teacher (often used when giving directions to support students in transitioning between activities) and a nurturing one (often used during direct instruction, small-group work, and when building relationships), as appropriate. In addition, as you set up the cultural norms of your classroom, you might teach students about the tone you choose to use and when choices are available to them. When setting expectations or giving directions, be sure to use a tone and language that *gets into every student's hearing*. How will you know? Every student will follow your directions!

"I Need to Earn Students' Respect"

No-Nonsense Nurturers recognize that in many classrooms, teachers earn students' respect by asserting authority in a firm, fair, and caring manner. Effective teachers understand the need to take charge of the classroom and provide strong and supportive guidance if they want students to respect them and follow their directions (Adkins-Coleman, 2010; Bondy & Ross, 2008; Bondy, Ross, Gallingane, & Hambacher, 2007; Brown, 2004; Delpit, 2006; Marzano & Marzano, 2003; Weiner, 1999; Wilson & Corbett, 2001). In addition, No-Nonsense Nurturers realize if they want to receive respect, they also need to give respect. They demonstrate respect by listening to student perspectives, asking questions while trying to eliminate their assumptions, and demonstrating and modeling respect to students as they would like to see it in their classrooms.

"100 Percent of My Students Can Be Engaged in Learning 100 Percent of the Time"

No-Nonsense Nurturers have a "by all means necessary" mentality. They work to learn from and understand the challenges their students face, but they do not allow those challenges to derail their high academic expectations. Instead, No-Nonsense Nurturers support and plan for obstacles that may arise for students. Let me share an example. As a student teacher, I knew one of my kindergarten students, Kyle, struggled every Monday morning. Having spent the weekend at his father's house and transitioning back to his mother's on Sunday night was difficult for Kyle. This made Monday mornings at schools stressful for him (and me). Planning for this became essential to his Monday morning success and the success of his classmates.

To accommodate his need for additional transition time, I worked with Kyle's mom. On Sunday evenings, she set up a ritual for Kyle to get ready for school (getting his backpack together, making choices for lunch, ensuring all homework was complete, and reading two books before bedtime). Then on Monday mornings,

Kyle's mother brought him to the classroom fifteen minutes earlier than the other students. While I finished getting ready for the day, Kyle told me about his weekend, the books he read with his mom the night before, and what special treat he had in his lunch. These small but very significant adjustments ensured Kyle's Monday mornings went far more smoothly.

No-Nonsense Nurturers believe getting an education is crucial to each student's future so they keep the bar for student achievement very high (Ferguson, 2008; Irvine & Fraser, 1998; Nieto, 2008; Wilson & Corbett, 2001). No-Nonsense Nurturers understand that the consequences of making excuses for students can create additional obstacles and result in fewer choices for students after high school.

Like all teachers, No-Nonsense Nurturers find some students more challenging than others to meet their goal of engaging 100 percent of students, 100 percent of the time. It is with these students they know they need to build the strongest relationships. These are the students who teach No-Nonsense Nurturers the most about their practice and what it really takes to reach everyone. These teachers understand how essential it is to take the extra time to figure out how to strengthen those relationships and learning tools for students who prove at the greatest risk of failure.

"I Listen to and Learn From My Students"

No-Nonsense Nurturers' ability to develop life-altering relationships that motivate students to reach high levels of academic achievement comes from listening to and learning from their students. When students are troubled or struggling, No-Nonsense Nurturers take the extra time to engage in and understand what is going on and see how they can help. No-Nonsense Nurturers focus on positive interactions with students by listening empathetically and providing empowering mentorship experiences.

"I Ensure Learning Is Relevant to Students' Lives"

No-Nonsense Nurturers do not shy away from topics that impact their students or communities, especially those who are historically disenfranchised. This often means conversations in their classrooms about poverty, race, and social injustice. No-Nonsense Nurturers take on these issues alongside their students to support everyone's learning, self-reflection, and examination of cultural biases. These masterful teachers realize when learning is relevant to their students' lives, it gives them a reason to want an education, make changes in their community, and fight against injustices they experience (Duncan-Andrade, 2007; Nieto, 2002; Paris & Alim, 2014; Picower, 2012). These classroom experiences give students tools to impact their lives and break cycles of oppression in their communities and beyond.

The No-Nonsense Nurturer Four-Step Model

As noted in the introduction, No-Nonsense Nurturers are teachers who set high expectations for themselves and their students. They create a consistent, trustworthy classroom that communicates high expectations, trust, and fairness. Additionally, they consistently develop life-altering relationships with students and leverage those connections to achieve high academic goals. They accomplish this by using the strategies of precise directions, positive narration, and accountability systems. These strategies lay the groundwork for developing relationships with all students, especially those historically marginalized in schools.

While the strategies of No-Nonsense Nurturers seem simple at first glance, they are quite nuanced and evolve over time through practice and feedback. As their skills develop and relationships flourish, No-Nonsense Nurturers facilitate critical thinking and support students in developing their voices both in the classroom and in the community.

Without question, building relationships with students is at the forefront of a No-Nonsense Nurturer's classroom management strategy. However, deep relationships take time to build, especially those that benefit both student and teacher. Therefore, to support students in their classrooms until they can form life-altering relationships, No-Nonsense Nurturers use specific strategies to set up classrooms where students feel supported, safe, and successful. These strategies make up the No-Nonsense Nurturer four-step model, which part 2 discusses in depth (see page 53). Figure 2.1 shows the No-Nonsense Nurturer four-step model.

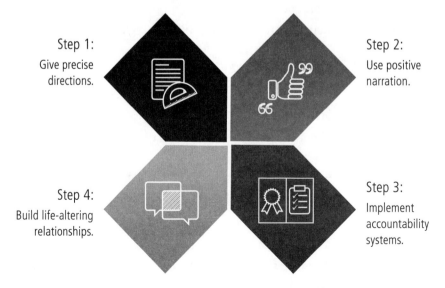

Figure 2.1: The No-Nonsense Nurturer four-step model.

Step 1: Give Precise Directions

Precise directions are the global positioning system (or GPS) for students navigating their classroom. Much like the GPS application you use on your smartphone to guide you to a new destination, students need precise directions with every new task or expectation in the classroom. Just like with a GPS, precise directions must be specific and timely and must lead students to success. When students find success in the classroom, it allows for opportunities to build relationships with their teacher and their peers.

Following is an example of precise directions: "When I say *go*, begin working with your shoulder partner in a library voice to solve problems one through ten on page 16 in your mathematics text. If you have a question, raise your hand and I will come to you. If you finish early, go back and check your answers. Go!"

Step 2: Use Positive Narration

After teachers give a direction, most of them notice students who are *not* doing what is being asked of them. These teachers must then make a decision on how to get all students on task and engaged. Should they call out the student in front of everyone? Ignore it? Approach the off-task student separately?

No-Nonsense Nurturers use an asset-based approach to classroom management by scanning the classroom and noticing out loud (positively narrating) students who are following directions. By narrating the components of the precise directions, a teacher provides examples of what all students should be doing, repeating the directions in a positive and supportive manner, and allowing students to self-regulate their choices. This, in return, creates positive momentum in the classroom and an opportunity for all students to hear (and see) the directions again and make a choice to engage before being held accountable for not following the directions.

Following is an example of positive narration: "Jayvon quickly turned to his shoulder partner. Kaitlyn and Diamond are discussing problem one in a library voice. David and José are solving problem two."

Step 3: Implement Accountability Systems

Accountability systems are important to No-Nonsense Nurturers to ensure consistency. Students earn consequences and incentives, and they give students opportunities to meet a teacher's expectations. No-Nonsense Nurturers have a goal of 100 percent engagement and give individualized consequences and collaborative incentives that result in a positive classroom learning environment.

Some teachers may think consequences are a form of punishment. No-Nonsense Nurturers don't see consequences that way; instead, they see consequences as a system that communicates they care too much about their students to let them be unsuccessful or make choices that don't serve them well. No-Nonsense Nurturers create a systematic, predictable accountability hierarchy that they teach students and implement fairly and consistently. This allows teachers to use consequences to set high expectations for students and demonstrate a heightened sense of care. If a student does not engage in a learning activity after precise directions and narration, No-Nonsense Nurturers care too much about their students to let them fail or not do what is expected of them; these teachers use an agreed-upon accountability hierarchy to hold students accountable for making good choices so they can be successful.

Following is an example of a consequence: "Susan, the directions are to work with your partner in a library voice. This is your warning for today. Turn to Robert and begin working on problem one. You've got this."

No-Nonsense Nurturers also allow students to earn incentives. After deciding on an incentive and class goals, all students work together, in a cooperative fashion, to earn a desired outcome.

Following is an example of an incentive: "Class, we have all been consistently working for seven minutes. You have just earned a class point. Keep up the good work!"

Step 4: Build Life-Altering Relationships

Rather than assume students know they care about them, No-Nonsense Nurturers go out of their way to prove just how much they care. Whether checking in on a family member, calling or visiting a student over the weekend, or attending a music recital, No-Nonsense Nurturers make sure students know how important they are inside and outside the classroom.

Maybe even more important, No-Nonsense Nurturers humanize themselves to their students. They tell stories about their own lives that are relevant to students' needs or a lesson. They apologize to students if they are wrong about something and share their interests, emotions, and life events. When we humanize ourselves as teachers, we support our relationships with students. When students see you as a person with thoughts, feelings, hopes, and dreams, you are establishing a culture of respect, dignity, and care that translates into a dynamic classroom with students who are willing to take risks, voice opinions, and learn from each other.

Following are two brief examples of building relationships.

"Charlene, I enjoyed attending part of your swim meet on Friday evening. Nice work on second place in the one-hundred-meter breaststroke! How did the rest of the meet go for you and the team?"

"Class, I messed up. Yesterday while I was working with Pablo, he pointed out to me that I have the wrong theorem listed for skill set 2.5. I went through our mathematics lab last night to make sure that was the only mistake in the lab. The mistake and correction are listed on the board. I know some of you have already worked on the problems associated with the theorem. This was my mistake. If you need an extra day to complete the assignment or help getting on the right track, please see me."

Conclusion

In the last two chapters, you read about three relationship-building paradigms—(1) unintended enablers, (2) negative controllers, and (3) No-Nonsense Nurturers. Nearly all teachers have slipped into and out of these relationship-building paradigms and teaching personas at one time or another. Even teachers, such as myself, who have demonstrated attributes of all these relationship paradigms still work hard each and every day to be an effective No-Nonsense Nurturer.

The next several chapters in part 2 will explore the No-Nonsense Nurturer four-step model that high-performing teachers use to create cultures of success in their classrooms.

Reflection Activities

The reflection activities on pages 48–52 are designed to help you reflect on your current professional practice and support your journey to becoming a No-Nonsense Nurturer. You may choose to complete them individually or in teams.

Reflect on Your
Relationship-Building Paradigms

Take ten to fifteen minutes to reflect on the following questions. Be honest with yourself so you can impact your own practice. Consider and reflect on the sentence stem activity you completed at the end of the introduction (page 13) and how it compares with your answers to the following questions.

What attributes of the ineffective relationship paradigms (unintended enabler or negative controller) do find yourself sometimes slipping in and out of? When does this usually happen for you?

When do you find you are most like a No-Nonsense Nurturer? What attributes of a No-Nonsense Nurturer come easily to you?

What motivations or attributes of No-Nonsense Nurturers do you most want to work on? How will you collect evidence of your progress in the goals you set?

Keep a Journal

We have all had No-Nonsense Nurturers as teachers. Take some time to journal about, reflect on, and discuss with a colleague a teacher who made a difference in your life.

How did this teacher impact you?

What did he or she do to support you academically and as a person?

How did this person shape you as an individual?

What qualities does he or she have that you would like to implement in your classroom tomorrow?

Examine Your Mindsets

It's possible that you are wrestling with some of the ideas this book presents. Maybe you are not entirely comfortable discussing class, culture, race, and the power dynamic between teachers and students. Perhaps you are realizing that despite your best intentions, some aspect of your teaching, mindset, or natural relationship-building paradigm is keeping you from effectively building the life-altering relationships that empower all students to excel, reduce stress, and increase your work satisfaction. If you are getting frustrated, *relax*. Self-reflection is difficult and takes practice. We all struggle with this, which means we are learning and challenging ourselves!

It's equally likely that many of the ideas in the book are true for you. You may be relieved to know other teachers have struggled, yet successfully established both the no-nonsense and nurturing approaches in their classrooms by reflecting on their practices, as you are doing here.

Before moving on, it is important to reflect on your beliefs and attitudes and better understand the ways your mindsets are empowering or disempowering you and your students. While no one becomes a teacher to hold students back from doing their best, somehow over time, certain mindsets surface subconsciously. Now is the time to reflect and make any necessary changes to ensure your classroom is set up for success.

Review each disempowering and empowering mindset in the following chart. Honestly note where you fall with a checkmark next to the mindset that best represents your thinking. Then, take a minute to reflect on and answer the questions. As you answer, note a next step you will take to shift to a more empowered mindset.

What do I believe about setting expectations for my students?

Disempowering	Empowering
I don't want to be mean or strict.	I need to be firm so my students know I care.
Mindset you want to work on (Are you working to improve the disempowering mindset, or are you eager to engage more often in the empowering mindset?)	

Who alone sets the tone for learning in my classroom and why does that matter?

One small step I will take to shift my mindset:

What do I believe about respect?

Disempowering	Empowering
Students should respect me because I am the teacher.	I need to earn students' trust and respect.
Mindset you want to work on (Are you working to improve the disempowering mindset, or are you eager to engage more often in the empowering mindset?)	
Who is primarily responsible for establishing a mutually respectful culture in my classroom? Why is such a culture critical to me and my students' success?	

page 2 of 3

One small step I will take to shift my mindset:

Do I believe *all* my students can achieve at high levels?

Disempowering	Empowering
I can't expect students with so many challenges to achieve at high levels.	My students can achieve if I set a high bar and provide the support they need to reach it.

Mindset you want to work on (Are you working to improve the disempowering mindset, or are you eager to engage more often in the empowering mindset?)

Who is primarily responsible for establishing high expectations in my classroom? Why are high expectations critical to me and my students' success?

One small step I will take to shift my mindset:

Every Student, Every Day © 2019 Kristyn Klei Borrero • SolutionTree.com
Visit **go.SolutionTree.com/behavior** to download this free reproducible.

PART 2

Establishing a No-Nonsense Nurturing Classroom Culture

CHAPTER 3

Give Precise Directions

No-Nonsense Nurturers understand that building life-altering relationships not only promotes high academic achievement for students but also creates high levels of job satisfaction for themselves. However, building these relationships takes time. To begin building these relationships, as previously noted, No-Nonsense Nurturers systematically integrate four distinct steps into their instructional practices: (1) give precise directions, (2) use positive narration, (3) implement accountability systems, and (4) build life-altering relationships. In this chapter, we'll dive into step one and investigate the importance of giving precise directions. See figure 3.1.

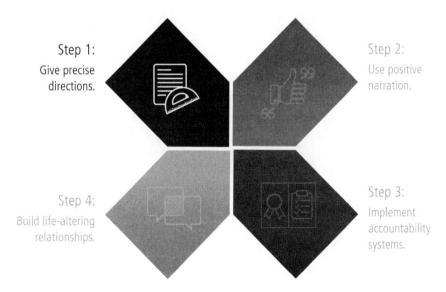

Figure 3.1: Give precise directions.

Your first reaction to this step may be, "Precise directions? Really? I give directions every day!" Teachers do give directions every day, but few teachers ever learned how to give directions precisely, concisely, and effectively. Believe it or not, there is actually a science to giving directions to students so they can be successful in your classroom. This chapter discusses the benefits of precise directions; guidelines for giving precise directions; precise directions as the key to policies, procedures, and routines; practice for perfect procedures and establishing a no-nonsense nurturing culture; and precise directions for students with additional needs.

While walking classrooms in a school in Charlotte, North Carolina, I got to observe two fourth-grade teachers teaching a reading lesson they had clearly collaborated in preparing. I was reminded of the importance of precise directions as students engaged in the activity.

Ms. Cabry set clear directions for the direct instruction part of her lesson: "Students, I have five minutes of material I want to teach you. In front of you, you have guided notes. As I work through the reading comprehension passage, I want you to fill in your guided notes silently and independently. If you have a question, write it on a sticky note, and I will answer it at the end of the passage." Ms. Cabry then moved through about four minutes of instruction flawlessly, reading through the passage and talking about her thinking and how she was making connections to the text to improve her comprehension. She and all twenty-six students in her class filled in their guided notes. Students' heads were bobbing in agreement, and students continually tracked her or the text she was reading.

Mr. Fox, however, struggled a bit more. Using the same text and guided notes as Ms. Cabry, his directions lacked precision: "Class, we have guided notes to fill in as I read this passage. Keep working as I read aloud." In his class, students struggled to follow along with him. Several students talked with their neighbors to try to figure out what to fill in on their guided notes, and two boys in the back of the room gave up about six minutes into the lesson and put their heads down on their desks. Mr. Fox's lesson took almost ten minutes to compete, and his engagement level was about 60 percent.

The biggest difference between the two lessons was how the teachers delivered their directions. While Ms. Cabry directed students on what to do and how they should engage in their learning, Mr. Fox's directions lacked clarity on how to engage in the activity, leaving several students guessing what to do or disengaging altogether. This resulted in almost half his class not paying attention and him taking more than twice the amount of time to get through the same amount of material.

From this example, it's clear how precise directions can benefit students in the classroom. Let's look at some of those benefits in more detail. Then, we will look at guidelines for giving precise directions, rules for No-Nonsense Nurturers, procedures for practicing precise directions, and addressing students with additional needs.

Benefits of Precise Directions

The first step in motivating students to quickly get on task and engaged is for you to communicate, in a no-nonsense manner, the precise directions you want them to follow. Precise directions are the road map to student success because they communicate what success *looks like* and *sounds like*. Students receive the opportunity to feel successful and to use their valuable learning time efficiently and effectively.

Many teachers give students directions for *what* to do, but they often leave out *how* to do it. Precise directions support students with the *what* and the *how* to do a task. Precise directions are also a simple way to start building relationships with students because a teacher who plans for student success is communicating to students that they matter.

To properly incorporate precise directions into your daily practice, design the directions in your lesson plans. The more clearly you outline directions for students, the more likely students will achieve success. After planning your directions for a week or so, you will get the hang of it; you might even eliminate the additional planning unless you are introducing a new procedure to the class.

Guidelines for Giving Precise Directions

In order to effectively communicate expectations for success to your students, do the following.

Tell Students What to Do and How to Do It

Teachers who are struggling with student behavior often fall into the trap of giving unclear (imprecise) directions. Why? Because many were never taught the importance of giving directions in the first place! As a result, some teachers only tell students *what* they want them to do. No-Nonsense Nurturers tell students what to do *and* how to do it. Consider the difference between vague and precise directions.

- Vague directions:
  - "Come in and begin writing in your journals."
  - "Begin working on your lab with your partner."

- Precise directions:
  - ▷ "Good morning! Enter the classroom in level zero, and go directly to your desks. Your journal prompt is on the board. Begin writing silently for five minutes, while I come around and check your homework, which should be placed in the top-right corner of your desk."
  - ▷ "Scholars, we are going to work in our groups to complete our science experiments. This means you will take fifteen seconds to move into your A groups using your level-one voices. You will then work for the next thirty minutes in your level-one voices to complete the lab. I will be walking around and checking in with groups to provide assistance when needed."

The problem with vague directions is that you are leaving it up to students to decide *how* they will follow your directions. Consequently, some students may choose to follow your directions in ways that are not in their best interest and may disrupt their classmates' learning.

Deliver Directions Using a Strong Teacher Voice

Just as important as *what* you tell the students to do is *how* you tell them to do it. No matter how precise your directions are, you'll most likely have students who will not listen unless you deliver the directions using your strong teacher voice (Bondy et al., 2007; Lemov, 2015). A *strong teacher voice* is a tone that gets into the hearing of every student (see chapter 2, page 40). It is your *I mean business* voice and posture. A strong teacher voice is never loud, nor does it require you to strain your voice.

When giving directions, do the following.

- **Have all the students' attention before beginning:** Make sure you have 100 percent attention before delivering directions. If needed, use an attention-getting signal (AGS) and then narrate (see chapter 4, page 87).

- **Stop and square up:** When giving directions, don't move around the room. Square up your shoulders and stand in front of the entire class so you can see all students, and they can all see you. Make eye contact with them. This body language sends the message that you have something important to say, and you expect students to follow your directions.

▶ **Use an economy of language:** When giving directions to students, the less you say, the more effective you will be. Too many words can communicate to students that you are unsure of what you really want, which can be confusing for students. To ensure an economy of language, design your directions while lesson planning.

Give MVP Directions

An easy way to determine what components your precise directions should include is to remember the acronym *MVP*. Precise directions communicate to students the movement, voice level, and participation you expect from them (Klei Borrero & Canter, 2018).

Movement

Inappropriate movement accounts for approximately 15 percent of the disruptive behavior in teachers' classrooms (Canter, 2010; Erdogan et al., 2010; Jones, 2000). This includes students getting out of their seats without permission, tapping their pencils, touching other students, running in the classroom, or using the restroom at inappropriate times. Thus, when you give directions, you must tell students precisely what movement is appropriate, as in the following examples.

▶ "Stay in your seat."

▶ "Walk directly to your seat."

▶ "Walk to the end of the line, and keep your hands to yourself."

▶ "Move with purpose and care into your collaborative groups."

Voice Level

It is very important to let students know the precise voice level or verbal behavior you expect in any activity. Studies note that at least 80 percent of the disruptive behavior in classrooms comes from inappropriate talking—students talking over the teacher, shouting out answers, or discussing an inappropriate topic during group work (Canter, 2010; Erdogan et al., 2010; Jones, 2000).

When you give directions, you must include the precise verbal behavior you expect, as in the following examples.

▶ "Complete the activity silently (level zero)."

▶ "Raise your hand, and wait to be called on before you speak."

▶ "Use your whisper voice."

- ▸ "Use level-one voices for group work."
- ▸ "When answering, use your presentation voice, or level-two voice."

An important cautionary note in regard to voice level is that teachers often confuse *quietly* with *silently* when they give directions. *Quietly* is a subjective term. What is quiet to the students may not be what is quiet to the teacher, and oftentimes when teachers use the term *quietly*, they are really asking for silence. *Silently* or *level zero* is specific and leaves no doubt about what behavior is expected.

For times when students are allowed to talk *quietly* during work time, teach them a whisper voice, inside voice, level-one voice, or twelve-inch voice. A *twelve-inch voice* is a voice level that only the people sitting next to you can hear and understand. By teaching students what these terms mean, you will communicate effectively the voice levels you expect.

At the beginning of the school year or when re-norming or resetting classroom expectations, most No-Nonsense Nurturers limit any talking that could disrupt the class. They ask students to enter the room without talking and expect silence during transitions. Silent movement, particularly at the beginning of the year, often cuts down on transition time, adding precious minutes to instructional lessons. Once students master transitions, most No-Nonsense Nurturers allow them to move in level-one or whisper voices to communicate and collaborate with one another during transitions. It is important to be intentional with your decisions about voice level and reflect on why you are asking for silence or why you are allowing talking.

Note that No-Nonsense Nurturers never want to limit students' purposeful *academic* verbal interactions during discussions or partner and group activities. Instead, they teach appropriate voice levels so successful academic discourse can occur. Student voice in the classroom is important and should be incorporated as frequently as possible to increase student engagement with one another.

Participation

For most academic activities, you must communicate *how* you want students to participate. Specifically, what do you want them to do with their brains?

- ▸ "Do your work independently."
- ▸ "Complete the assignment, and then read your free-reading book."
- ▸ "Discuss the assigned topic with your group."
- ▸ "Review sections one through three of the lab assignment with your lab partner."

You don't have to give your directions in MVP order; this acronym is just to help you remember all parts of your directions. (Some teachers, including myself, tend to give the voice-level directions last, because it accounts for up to 80 percent of off-task behaviors and, to be honest, it's the part I tend to forget.) Give all parts of your directions in a way that supports you and your students' learning.

As students begin to demonstrate mastery of classroom procedures and routines, you can shorten your directions by using an adverb for the directions related to movement, voice, or participation, as in the following examples.

- ▸ "Move directly to your seat and begin your partner shares in level-one voices."

- ▸ "Silently track me when I speak."

Provide Time Frames

Some No-Nonsense Nurturers are also explicit regarding the amount of time students should spend on a particular assignment or activity. Many teachers plan for the time frame to keep themselves on track. Using a timer for activities helps keep students on track. Some examples of directions with specific time frames include the following.

- ▸ **Transition:** "Students, when I say *go*, you have thirty seconds to put your journals away and get your mathematics materials out silently. This should all be done at your desk. Go!"

- ▸ **Group work:** "In your small groups, you have twenty-five minutes to complete activities one and two in your mathematics lab. Do this using level-one voices, and only materials managers may move about the classroom to retrieve materials. Questions? You may begin."

Check for Understanding

At the beginning of the year or after introducing a new procedure or routine, check for understanding to ensure students received and understood your directions. During this check, consider calling on students who have a tendency to be off task during the activity. There are two reasons to do this.

1. You want to make sure students heard and understood your directions.

2. You want students to know that you are paying attention to them, thus dramatically reducing the likelihood they will get off task or not follow your directions.

The following are examples of questions to check for understanding.

▸ "Are there any questions about the directions we are to follow during the next five minutes?"

▸ "We are now moving into our mathematics centers. What voice level are we in, Cesar?"

▸ "What are the three most important things to remember about the directions I just gave for small-group work? Give me one, Caroline."

Cue Students to Start

Finally, make sure to establish *when* students are to start following your directions. Some of your highest-achieving students will want to begin working before the directions are complete. This can take away from the learning environment of those students who need to hear all your directions to be successful. So, you want to establish a cue that indicates when students should start moving. For example: "When I say *go*, you will start lining up."

If this feels like a lot, it isn't. It just takes practice. Stand in front of a mirror—square up and shoulders back. Now practice out loud some of the following precise directions while looking in the mirror. This provides strong practice for when you get up in front of your class.

▸ **Classroom entrance:** "When I welcome you in, silently enter the classroom. Go immediately to your seats and begin working on the Do Now lists I have placed on your desks for the next seven minutes. Welcome in!"

▸ **Teacher-directed instruction:** "When I'm teaching, you should silently track me, following along on your paper, while staying seated. Be sure you write what I write on the board in your notes. If you have a question, raise a silent hand, and I will be sure to call on you."

▸ **Whole-class discussion:** "During our discussion, silently raise your hand and wait to be called on. Track the speaker, and when speaking, use your presentation voice."

▸ **Partner work:** "When I say *go*, begin working with your shoulder partner, stay seated, and use your twelve-inch voice to complete activity seventeen in your literature text. You have ten minutes. Go!"

Use figure 3.2 as a cheat sheet when designing your precise directions during lesson planning.

Step	Reason	Examples
Stop and square up.	Demonstrates importance of your directions	Move to the front of the classroom, square shoulders, and look students in the eyes as you give directions.
Use a strong teacher voice.	Demonstrates a new activity or transition and the need for all students to pay attention in order to be successful	Firm, strong voice with a low yet commanding volume
Give an attention-getting signal.	Gets all students' attention so they are able to receive directions	Call and response Chime Rhythmic clapping
Give MVP directions with time frames, if needed. • Movement • Voice level • Participation • Time frame	Provides students with the *what* and *how* to be successful for the transition or activity	"In level-one voices, move directly to your lab station and begin the first three sections of the lab with your group. I will set a timer for thirty minutes for you to complete the activity. If you have any questions, raise your hand and I will support your group." (Consider tone and economy of language.)
Check for understanding.	Ensures everyone understands expectations when you give new or complicated directions	"How long will we be working on this lab, Christian?" "What sections are we to complete, Kendra?" "What's our voice level, Ryan?"
Cue students to start.	Ensures students listen to all parts of the directions to promote success	"You may begin." "Go!"

Figure 3.2: Steps for designing and delivering precise directions.

*Visit **go.SolutionTree.com/behavior** for a free reproducible version of this figure.*

Precise Directions as the Key to Policies, Procedures, and Routines

From the first day of school, No-Nonsense Nurturers lay the foundation for life-altering relationships with students by establishing a mutually respectful, no-nonsense yet nurturing classroom culture that promotes high expectations, academic achievement, and personal growth. But how do you begin doing that?

An often unrecognized attribute that contributes to these teachers' success is the time and effort they put into teaching their policies, procedures, and routines when the school year starts or when they need to reset or re-norm classroom expectations (Bondy et al., 2007; Farr, 2010). Rather than just jumping into teaching academic content, No-Nonsense Nurturers realize that solid routines and procedures serve academics and, more importantly, students. If taught well, policies and procedures can save the teachers and students precious time during the school year. Like No-Nonsense Nurturers, high-performing teachers spend the majority of the first week or two of school ensuring all students master the policies, procedures, and routines in the context of academic content (Klei Borrero & Canter, 2018). This promotes a positive classroom experience throughout the entire school year. So, what is the key to solid policies, procedures, and routines? Precise directions!

Choose Classroom Policies, Procedures, and Routines

There are myriad classroom activities, policies, procedures, and routines, ranging from how students enter the classroom, to how they should stay engaged during instructional activities, to how they transition between activities and out of class. Take time to think about and list every possible activity or transition you will do repeatedly in your classroom. For each of these, you must teach a policy, procedure, or routine. Each of these routines calls for a set of precise directions. For elementary teachers, the list can be twenty to thirty; for middle and high school teachers, the list is typically about fifteen or more necessary policies, procedures, and routines. Table 3.1 (page 65) notes common policies, procedures, and routines you will likely need to implement in your classroom.

This list is not exhaustive, and you may choose to teach your policies, procedures, and routines differently, but these will get you started down the right path.

Table 3.1: Policies, Procedures, and Routines to Consider Planning for Your Classroom

Elementary Classrooms	Middle and High School Classrooms
Transitioning from class to class	Transitioning from class to class
Arriving in the morning	Entering the class
Dismissing for the afternoon	Turning in homework
Taking restroom breaks	Exiting the class
Lining up	Taking restroom breaks
Contacting the teacher	Contacting the teacher
Moving from the rug to desks	Retrieving materials
Giving instructional activities	Giving instructional activities
Retrieving materials	Conducting lab procedures
Turning in homework	Assigning Do Nows
Turning in classwork	Giving exit tickets
Assigning Do Nows	Passing out papers
Giving exit tickets	Using technology
Cleaning up after an activity	Conducting fire or emergency drills
Assigning class jobs	
Using technology	
Conducting fire or emergency drills	

Teach and Practice Policies, Procedures, and Routines

No-Nonsense Nurturers do much more than just announce policies, procedures, and routines to their students. They teach students *why* the policies, procedures, and routines are important as well as *how* to follow them using guidelines such as scripting precise directions and giving students opportunities to practice them to meet the objectives (Ross et al., 2008). Following are some strategies for teaching practice policies, procedures, and routines to students.

Plan

Engage in lesson planning to teach behavioral expectations the first time you engage in a class activity, instructional strategy, policy, procedure, or routine. Teach students how you expect them to behave and move through the activity. Script your precise directions. In the beginning of the year, create and execute lesson plans for how you will teach every policy, procedure, and routine you plan to use in your classroom.

Introduce a Rationale for Your Expectations

Your students are much more likely to meet your expectations when you explain why following your precise directions is in their best interest. Identify the benefits for them as individual students and as a class. For example:

▶ "Students, today I am going to teach you our lab procedure. We will use this procedure all year to keep each of us safe and so we can use our time wisely as we navigate our way through AP chemistry."

▶ "As a class, we will use guided notes to support our learning during guided instruction and as a reference while solving problems and studying for your quizzes and tests. Follow along as I introduce this important practice so we can use it to support your learning throughout the year."

▶ "Aspiring first graders, we will transition to the carpet several times a day. We don't want to waste too much time doing this because we have lots of learning to do this year in kindergarten. We are going to practice this procedure so everyone moves quickly and safely and we get plenty of time to learn how to read this year!"

Describe the Behaviors You Expect to See and Hear

Communicate your expectations clearly so students know exactly what to do to be successful. Use your precise directions and positive narration (see chapter 4, page 87) to ensure success with new routines. For example:

▶ "The first page of your lab will always include any needed safety procedures. Every Tuesday and Wednesday are lab days in AP chemistry. When you enter the room, move directly to the back cubbies and place your backpack and other unnecessary materials in the cubicles. Pick up your lab and make your way directly to your lab station. Take a seat on your stool and begin reading the safety procedures silently and independently on page one of the lab."

▶ "Take guided notes while I am teaching you a new concept. While I am teaching, you should be silently tracking me or your guided notes, following along to write in necessary information to support your study habits. If you have a question during direct instruction, please ask. Raise your hand, and I will call on you."

▶ "Kindergarteners, we are going to learn step one of three to move to the carpet. When I say *go*, everyone will stand up and silently push in their chairs. Stand behind your chair and track me for step two. Go!"

Demonstrate the Procedure

Consider having students demonstrate, model, or role-play what it looks and sounds like to appropriately respond during the activity, procedure, or routine. Narrate the appropriate student behaviors as students demonstrate the procedure. In addition, consider having students role-play what it should *not* look and sound like, and critique the procedure, if appropriate for your grade level.

Check for Understanding

Make sure all students understand how to succeed with each expectation for the activity, procedure, or routine you are teaching. With commonly used routines, especially in high school lab settings, some teachers provide a quiz so students can demonstrate their mastery of the procedure or routine.

▶ "What is the first thing you do on lab days? Lola?"

▶ "Why is it important that we use guided notes? Hector?"

▶ "Who can show me step one for making our way to the carpet? Table 2, please demonstrate this for the class."

No-Nonsense Nurturers and Rules

No-Nonsense Nurturers don't spend a lot of time on classroom rules. Some make contracts with their students about expectations, while others state their rules in a positive manner generic enough to support and guide students in any classroom situation. The following are some examples of classroom rules. When introducing them, be sure to let students know that you don't create rules to penalize or restrict them, but rather to provide a safe environment where everyone can thrive and feel safe.

▶ "Follow all directions."

▶ "Keep hands and feet to yourself."

▶ "Demonstrate care and respect for others, the materials, and expectations in our classroom."

▶ "Be prepared with your assignments, and demonstrate your growth mindset."

Perfect Practice Makes Perfect Procedures

Note these words of wisdom from legendary football coach Vince Lombardi (n.d.): "Practice does not make perfect. Only perfect practice makes perfect." If No-Nonsense Nurturers teach appropriate behavior for an activity, but later students do not meet the expectations, these teachers ask students to practice the activity again until they *all* perform it perfectly (Lemov, 2010; Ross et al., 2008). Perfect practice does not mean penalizing students if they don't get it right the first time. Rather, this is a chance for you to introduce class incentives (see chapter 5, page 132) and reflect on how you can provide more precise directions and opportunities for students to succeed.

Precise directions are the key to solid policies, procedures, and routines in your classroom. Drive classroom routines with precise directions—if students know what to do, when to do it, and how to do it, they will be far more successful. The following sections note a few examples of perfect procedures that you should consider for your classroom.

Entrance to the Classroom

The most important moment in any school day is when students first enter your classroom. If students are allowed to enter your classroom in a rowdy, disruptive manner and do not immediately get to work, you are sending the message that it is okay to waste valuable learning time. On the other hand, if you expect students to enter the room silently (or using level-one voices) and purposefully get right to work, you are sending the message that you are so committed to their education that you will not allow them to squander any opportunity for learning. Whatever message you send to your students in the first few minutes of class is likely to carry over throughout the period or day.

Take the lead from No-Nonsense Nurturers and set up tight procedures to ensure you are sending a message of high expectations when students enter the classroom. Following are some strategies you can use to let students know the correct way to enter the classroom.

Communicate Expectations for Entering the Classroom

As students enter, quickly state your precise directions: "Walk to your desks silently, sit down, and begin your Do Now independently."

It is important to note that during the first week of school or when re-norming your classroom culture, you may not want to greet students at the door. Greeting students is a great instinct because you want to create a warm, caring, and welcoming environment. However, consider holding off on welcoming students until you have established this procedure. Instead, consider standing in front of the class to monitor and give feedback to students on how they are meeting your expectations for entering the classroom and getting to work. This helps ensure students understand the procedure to come in and immediately get to work, and you won't feel as overwhelmed as you solidify the procedure.

After a week or so and after you establish the procedure, stand at the door and add an additional layer of multitasking to your routine by greeting students. As you stand at the door to greet students, check in, and build relationships, students will have already developed some automaticity with the procedure and you can multitask through this time.

Implement a Beginning-of-Class Routine

It's important for students to know exactly what they should do the moment they enter your classroom. Teachers should consider the following.

▸ **Have students pick up or access their assignments or activities:** If you give out assignments or worksheets, they should be located on a table by the door where students enter. Teach students to check the table when they enter the room and pick up a packet on the way to their desks. If students are expected to access their assignments on Google Drive or another online application, teach the procedure for getting out computers and getting right to work.

▸ **Establish a homework submission routine:** If students have homework due, they need to know what to do with it upon entering your classroom. Many teachers have a dedicated spot where students can place it (such as on a table or on the corner of their desks). Other teachers choose to have students submit their homework assignments electronically. Intentionally plan what works best for you, and keep in mind the flow of your classroom and any other logistics that could be potential barriers to a fluid process.

▸ **Move with purpose:** Teach students through your precise directions that everything they do on the way into your classroom has a procedure and specific expectations. Movement through the classroom should be quick and safe.

▸ **Set a beginning-of-class procedure:** Provide students with precise directions at the beginning of class time, such as the following.

▷ "Without talking, pick up today's assignments, drop off your homework, go directly to your seats, and begin your Do Now. It's great to have you here today!'"

▷ "Using your library voices, quickly pick up your Do Now and get out your homework. You have forty-five seconds to be in your seats and silently working on the four mathematics problems on the front board. I'm looking forward to our lesson today."

▷ "Good morning! Computers are in their charging stations. Purposefully enter, retrieve your computer, and log in to our Google Drive. Your Do Now is uploaded, and you have seven minutes to silently complete it. After completing it, be sure to double-check that your homework assignment is in the homework folder on our classroom drive. Our lab will begin in eight minutes. The timer is set. Let's get started!"

▸ **Have a Do Now assignment at the start of every class:** Your goal is to impress upon your students that you do not want to waste one minute of learning time. Thus, you want to have an assignment on the board, in Google Drive, or on a handout for students to complete as soon as they are seated. This enables students to start work even though you may still be greeting their peers or taking care of other business at the beginning of class. The Do Now assignment should meet the following criteria.

▷ It should require students to produce a written product—for example, answering three to five questions so you can check and use as a formative assessment.

▷ Because you can use this assignment as a formative assessment to gauge learning from the previous day and students' background knowledge, have students complete the Do Now independently—without your help or help from classmates.

▷ It should include a review of the previous day's learning as well as preview questions for the day's lesson so you can determine how much students might already know about what you are going to teach.

- ▸ Include one to two questions reviewing yesterday's lesson. This checks students' retention of a concept.
- ▸ Include one to two questions previewing what students will be learning in class that day. Students might not get these correct, but the questions will inform you about student background knowledge, alert students to the learning targets for the day, and help establish the day's learning goal.

▷ You can use Do Nows to introduce the day's activities and learning objectives in a culturally relevant fashion, engaging students' interest immediately.

Transitions

Transitions are those times when students move from one activity to another or from one location to another. Transitions can often be difficult for teachers to manage because of the number of students in their classrooms. In addition, an enormous amount of time is often wasted when transitions do not go smoothly.

Many teachers have ten or more transitions per day. If you could cut just one minute from each transition and sustain that over 180 school days, you could accrue up to thirty hours of instructional time, which is almost one week of instruction!

No-Nonsense Nurturers know that the more tightly choreographed and practiced the transitions are, the quicker they can be completed, leaving more time for learning. The following are some guidelines for efficient transitions.

Keep Transitions as Quiet as Possible

No-Nonsense Nurturers expect their students to be purposeful when they engage in any transition. For some transitions, like moving to the carpet or lining up for lunch, this may mean remaining silent throughout the process. For other transitions, such as cleaning up after an activity or getting ready to change classes, this may mean using level-one or library voices. No-Nonsense Nurturers do not place these stipulations on transitions to be rigid or overly strict; they do so because it is challenging to manage all students moving at once, and more effective and efficient to limit talking (especially at the beginning of the year) during transitions. For example: "Young scholars, we need to move into our partner groups. Gather your materials and silently and swiftly move to these groups in thirty seconds. Go!"

Scaffold Complex Directions

When developing precise directions that are also concise, many teachers realize their previous directions were often too long and complicated to follow, especially for younger students. Teaching policies, procedures, and routines can be complex, so you may need to scaffold your precise directions.

For example, some teachers might say to their students, "I want you to come to the rug, so stand up, push in your chairs, then walk to the rug. When you are at the rug, I want you to sit crisscross applesauce, and do all of this without talking."

These directions may be too complicated for younger students to follow and will simply lead to wasted time and frustration for both students and teacher. Let's look at some ways to scaffold these directions.

Chunk or Divide Directions Into Distinct, Numbered Steps

Using the previous example of moving from seats to the rug, you might teach students the following.

▸ "When I say *one*, silently stand up and push in your chairs."

▸ "When I say *two*, silently walk directly to your rug spot and stand."

▸ "When I say *three*, silently sit down crisscross applesauce."

▸ "One. Javion stood up silently. Ciara pushed in her chair. Thomas pushed in his chair and stood behind it."

▸ "Two. Marquell is walking silently to the rug. Aria is standing on her spot without talking. David found his spot on the rug."

▸ "Three. Evan sat down immediately on his spot. Sarah is silently sitting crisscross applesauce. Aquila sat down quickly without talking."

When you give directions in this way, students can move step-by-step through the transition, ensuring efficiency and fluidity, and that they will be able to reach mastery quickly.

High school lab, music, and art teachers often have complex sets of directions to complete extended activities. At the beginning of the class, review all steps of the activity using visuals, but then type or write all directions on note cards for students to use during learning time.

Transition to Another Activity While Remaining Seated

Seated transitions tend to be easier for students and teachers because there is limited movement in the classroom, but there is still opportunity for wasted time. You can use the previously stated strategy of breaking down the steps, as in the following.

▸ "When I say *one*, silently put away the materials from our mathematics lesson."

▸ "When I say *two*, silently take your reading folder and guided reading book out of your desk and place it on top of your desk."

▸ "When I say *three*, silently track me, showing me you are ready to begin literacy circles."

Or you can give a set of directions like the following.

▸ "When I say *go*, with your twelve-inch voice, put away your mathematics materials and get out your reading folder and guided reading book, and place them on your desk. You have thirty seconds to complete this task. When you are ready, silently track me so I know you are ready to begin literacy circles. Go!"

Line Up or Leave the Classroom

Transitions to leave the classroom can be most stressful for teachers. The following is an example of how to break down directions so students successfully move from one part of the school to the next.

▸ "When I say *one*, silently stand up and push in your chairs."

▸ "When I say *two*, line up silently, facing the door."

▸ "When I say *three*, silently move through the hallway to gym class. Everybody is expected to follow the line leader and keep their hands to themselves."

▸ "Middle schoolers, that is the bell. As you clean up to leave, keep out your assignment from today and hand it to me on your way out.

Remember, chapter 22 is due tomorrow. Exit the classroom using a level-one voice. Great class today. Have a good one!"

▶ "Juniors, the bell will ring in five minutes. Remember, I dismiss you, the bell does not dismiss you. During the last few minutes of class, stay in your seat and silently complete your exit ticket from the day's learning. After the bell rings, I will dismiss you and collect your exit tickets on the way out. Begin."

Have Students Move From Point to Point

Another challenge for many teachers is trying to get their classes to move in line outside the classroom. Consider using another scaffolding strategy; have the students walk from one location to another and then stop and wait for directions to move again.

▶ "When I say *go*, silently walk in a straight line to the stairs and stop. Then I will tell you when to go down the stairs. Go."

▶ "Make your way safely down the stairs and to the door of our classroom. Remain silent so we don't disrupt the learning of other scholars. Jamey, please lead us down the steps."

By having students walk from one point to another, you can keep them closer to you and narrate their behaviors more frequently. As students master walking in the halls, make the points farther from one another to quicken the transitions.

Time the Transitions

Your goal should always be to make transitions as efficient as possible. One trick many No-Nonsense Nurturers use to pick up the pace of transitions is timing them with a stopwatch. Challenge students to improve their time by making it a game, as in the following.

▶ "Our record for cleaning up and lining up is fifty-three seconds. Let's see if you can beat that today."

▶ "Yesterday, we completed our exit procedures in two minutes and fifteen seconds. When I say *go*, clean up your area, retrieve your backpack, and get packed up to leave. You may use your level-one voice, but stay focused. We are shooting for less than two minutes to complete our end-of-day procedure. Go!"

Attention-Getting Signals

One of the very first procedures you need to teach students is the signal you will use when you want their complete attention. It is important to note that any attention-getting signal is a code for a precise direction. When you give this signal, you are telling students to stop what they are doing and silently track you for a set of directions. Treat your AGS like a precise direction. In other words, narrate the expectation explicitly after you give the signal if you do not have 100 percent of students following the expectation. Typical AGSs include the following.

Choral Response

For choral response, the teacher begins with a word or phrase prompting students to respond in unison.

> **Teacher:** "Princeton!" (name of school)
>
> **Students:** "Vikings!" (mascot)
>
> **Narrate:** "Vynesha has her eyes on me and is silent. Carrie froze immediately. William put his pencil down."

Hand Signal

Raise one hand in the air, and put one finger on your lips in the "shh!" sign.

> **Narrate:** "Vynesha has her eyes on me and is silent. Carrie froze immediately. William put his pencil down."

Rhythmic Clapping

Establish a routine where you clap several times and then have all the students join in. After the clapping, narrate expectations.

> **Narrate:** "Vynesha has her eyes on me and is silent. Carrie froze immediately. William put his pencil down."

Specific Sounds

Ring a bell, clap two sticks together, or hit a chime.

> **Narrate:** "Vynesha has her eyes on me and is silent. Carrie froze immediately. William put his pencil down."

Routine Language to Support Precise Directions

You will use certain routines often in the classroom. Teach students these routines so you can easily refer to them during your precise directions. Some examples include the following.

STAR or SPARK

If students aren't ready to learn when you're teaching, you're simply wasting your time. That is why No-Nonsense Nurturers make it a priority to teach how they expect students to react during instructional time.

You can teach the acronyms STAR or SPARK, or come up with your own!

STAR

Sit up.

Track the speaker.

Ask and answer questions.

Respect classmates around you.

SPARK

Sit up.

Pay attention.

Ask and answer questions.

Respond.

Keep tracking.

STAR and *SPARK* are great shorthand methods to get students on task when you're teaching or having a class discussion.

Voice Levels

As noted previously, many No-Nonsense Nurturers establish specific voice levels to use throughout the year. My favorite is a voice-level chart posted in the front of the room as an artifact after you have taught it to the class.

- **Voice-level zero:** Silence; used for independent work
- **Voice-level one:** Whisper voice; used for partner work or group work
- **Voice-level two:** Presentation voice; used for answering questions, presenting, or teaching

Directions After Establishing a No-Nonsense Nurturing Culture

After you have taught your routines, policies, and procedures, and students fully understand and consistently comply with the associated precise directions, you will be able to shorten your directions.

For example, during independent work assignments, you gave students the following precise direction: "Silently, work on the assignment, stay in your seat, and raise your hand for help. If you finish early, check your answers and then read from your guided reading book."

At some point in the school year, you notice 100 percent of your students are consistently on task and engaged during independent work time. Now all you might have to say is: "When I say *go*, you will move into independent work time." These few words will be sufficient to clearly communicate your expectations to students because they have mastered the independent work time procedure.

I can't emphasize enough how much precise directions help support your classroom. When planning and designing precise directions, you can use them to monitor your own definitions of success and what it looks like. Many teachers report that when planning precise directions, they also take the opportunity to tighten up their lessons because this extra step in planning challenges them on what they really want students to get from their learning that day.

Equally important is that precise directions provide students with the structure for how to find success in your classroom. Success breeds additional success, and many students who were once disruptive or struggled to achieve in your classroom because of unclear expectations will likely become more engaged. By setting the standard and being clear with your directions, disruptions will decrease considerably, allowing for more instructional time and decreasing your frustration level.

Precise Directions for Students With Additional Needs

The No-Nonsense Nurturers we studied have *inclusionary classes*. This means that although these teachers taught in general education classrooms, all included students with 504 plans and individualized education programs (IEPs). Some of the classrooms we have studied had 40 percent or more students with programs or plans (Klei Borrero & Canter, 2018).

When entering a No-Nonsense Nurturer's classroom, it is often hard to discern which students need accommodations because 100 percent are meeting both behavioral and academic expectations. However, during interviews, No-Nonsense Nurturers were keenly aware of and well-versed in students' 504 plans or IEPs. Not only did No-Nonsense Nurturers implement the necessary intervention team strategies but they also advocated for students when they felt the students had met their 504 or IEP goals or needed to set additional or different goals (Klei Borrero & Canter, 2018).

All educators are legally (and morally) obligated to follow 504 plans and IEPs and serve any student they feel might have additional needs. However, if you believe something in one of these plans or programs is not supporting a student you serve, you have the right to call a meeting to provide input and ideas for the best accommodations for the student.

Precise directions are the guide to success for *all* students, especially those who have additional needs. Students who find engaging in academic work challenging or who feel overwhelmed when adapting to appropriate behaviors need precise directions to ensure their success.

While necessary, your precise directions might change slightly to accommodate students with additional needs. For example, the student's plan might require you to post directions with visuals or use nonverbal cues to support common classroom policies, procedures, and routines. Your economy of language for students with speech or processing concerns is important so they can interpret all parts of your directions. Consider more practice for students who need accommodations or nonverbal cues indicating a transition or a common precise direction in your classroom. Remember, as you plan with other teachers that support you and students with additional needs, you are obligated to include these accommodations for the identified students. However, you may want to consider using these accommodations for your entire class. Many students can benefit from them, and the students needing the accommodations will not feel excluded if you use them with everyone. These additional steps or accommodations are likely to support all learners in your classroom.

Conclusion

This chapter discussed step one of the No-Nonsense Nurturer four-step model: give precise directions. Precise directions support you and your students for success because you deliver a clear expectation for learning. In addition, precise directions are key for establishing key policies, procedures, and routines in your classroom. By teaching routines, you waste less time and allot more time for learning and engagement. Once well established, policies, procedures, and routines provide safety and structure that support your classroom throughout the year.

This first step of the four-step model is a foundational piece for building relationships with your students, as precise directions provide opportunities for all students to succeed. The next chapter explores positive narration and how this No-Nonsense Nurturer strategy supports your precise directions and high expectations, and deepens relationships in your classroom.

▶ Video

This brief video montage was designed for readers to view the steps of the No-Nonsense Nurturer four-step model individually and in teams. Scan this code to view No-Nonsense Nurturers as they demonstrate precise directions in action.

Precise Directions in Action

www.ct3education.com/book/precise-directions

✎ Reflection Activities

The reflection activities on pages 80–85 are designed to help you reflect on your current professional practice and support your journey to becoming a No-Nonsense Nurturer. You may choose to complete them individually or in teams.

Write Precise Directions on Sticky Notes

Giving precise directions consistently allows students to know exactly what to do and how to do it. However, it takes concerted effort and practice to make your directions precise, strong, and effective.

Scripting precise directions for common procedures, jotting them on sticky notes, and keeping them handy for reference throughout the day is a dynamic way to start building efficacy in your directions.

Try scripting precise directions on sticky notes. Challenge yourself to write at least six different sets of directions. A great way to check that your directions are precise and concise is to ensure each direction can fit on a three-inch × three-inch sticky note. You can assume directions are too long if you find yourself struggling to get it on all one small note!

The following is an example of a sticky note.

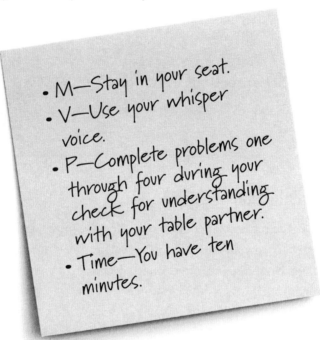

Once you have your sticky notes, practice saying these directions in front of the mirror in a strong yet natural teacher voice. The previous sticky note example might sound like the following: "Students, nice work with the guided practice. We are now going to work with our table partners in a whisper voice on problems one through four in your check for understanding. You have ten minutes, and you are to stay in your seats. Begin."

Break the Code for Precise Directions

The graphic organizer on pages 82–83 contains information from this chapter about designing and using precise directions. It seems like a lot, but it really isn't when you get used to it. Using the notes and examples, plan several sets of precise directions and write them in the second column. Remember to be as brief as possible. Once completed, practice saying your precise directions in front of the mirror and then in the car on your way to work. Perfect practice promotes perfect delivery, and far more of your students will be on task and engaged!

Type	Directions	Example	Notes
Tell students what to do and how to do it using a strong teacher voice and an attention-getting signal (AGS).		Ring a bell.	The AGS is a code for precise directions. You will need to explicitly teach this to students, as you will use it often to get their attention.
Identify movement.		"Turn to your partner."	What are students doing with their bodies?
Identify voice level.		"In voice-level one . . . "	What are students doing with their mouths?
Identify participation.		"Discuss two character traits for the main character and how you anticipate they will affect the plot."	What are students doing with their brains?

Provide a time frame.	"You have four minutes."	Think about how much time is necessary for students to complete this task.
Explain what students should do when they are done.	"Silently log your and your partner's ideas in your character journal."	Depending on how much time there is, you may want students to sit silently but be cognizant of wasting time.
Check for understanding.	"What is the voice level, student A? What are we discussing, student B? How much time do we have, student C?"	Once the check for understanding is complete, say *go* to get students started, and immediately narrate about students getting to work.
Cue students to start.	"When I say go . . ." "When I welcome you in . . ."	This is important so students don't start moving until all your directions are completed.

Reflect on Your Routines

Reflect on your classroom routines.

Which routines are currently working?

Are they quick?

Do they ensure all students are safe?

Is there something you could do to tighten up certain transitions?

Consider rethinking one of your routines. How will you improve it tomorrow? Script your precise directions.

Plan Your Policies, Procedures, and Routines

Classroom routines are the foundation for ensuring there is plenty of time for learning. Table 3.1 (page 65) includes policies, procedures, and routines you will likely need to introduce into your classroom. Decide which are the most important to introduce immediately and plan for two of them. Be sure to plan precise directions and narrations for each policy and procedure.

CHAPTER 4

Use Positive Narration

I n the first step of the four-step model, No-Nonsense Nurturers communicate the precise directions students must follow to be successful in the classroom. The next step is to motivate students to follow these directions by using positive narration.

Take a moment to think about what you do *after* you deliver a set of directions. If you are like most teachers, you scan the room to seek out those students who are *not* following your directions, thus focusing on what isn't happening in the classroom instead of all the good work that is happening.

No-Nonsense Nurturers take the opposite approach. After giving a set of directions, they scan the class to narrate (or notice out loud) students who *are* following directions, focusing on the positive first and highlighting those students. In this chapter, we focus on this positive narration. See figure 4.1.

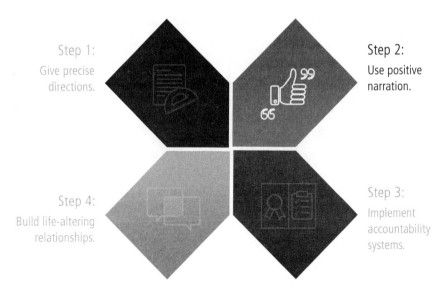

Figure 4.1: Use positive narration.

Positive narration creates a positive class momentum while highlighting what to do instead of what focusing on what not to do. Here is an example.

- **Precise directions:** "When I say *go* in a level-one voice, turn to your shoulder partner and discuss the three main causes of the French Revolution. Go!"

- **Positive narration:** "Jackie has turned to face her partner. Kiah is using her level-one voice. Max is discussing one of the main causes of the French Revolution."

Please note, in the preceding narrations, the teacher is not praising the students, but merely noticing out loud what students are doing that correlates with the directions. (For more on praise versus narration, see page 90.) In this chapter, we will discuss the benefits of positive narration, how positive narration supports student behavior, and positive narration for students with additional needs.

Benefits of Positive Narration

Research shows positive narration as one of the more powerful strategies No-Nonsense Nurturers use with their students to get them on task and to keep them engaged (Klei Borrero & Canter, 2018; Mixon, 2012). Let's examine some of the benefits of using this strategy.

Creates Positive Momentum

After giving directions to students, your response to their actions profoundly impacts the type of momentum you create in your classroom. Less effective teachers tend to immediately respond to those students who are off task or disruptive. This affirms that *not* following directions is the norm, which establishes a negative momentum in the classroom.

No-Nonsense Nurturers put a great deal of effort into noticing students who *are* following directions. This sets up the expectation that in these classrooms, the norm is for students to follow every direction. The resulting positive momentum reduces teachers' stress and improves the learning environment for all students. Simple, yet brilliant!

To illustrate this, consider the following narrations and which you would rather hear as a student.

- **Ineffective teacher after giving directions:** "John Michael, you are supposed to be working in your journal. Get to work."

▸ **No-Nonsense Nurturer after giving directions:** "Kevin is writing in his journal. Kendra is working on her journal entry." (After hearing the first two narrations, John Michael realizes what he is supposed to be doing.) "John Michael is silently writing in his journal."

If you were a student, chances are you would feel more empowered with the second example. It is positive, even soothing, and gives students a chance to catch their breath, observe other students engaging in precise directions, and make the choice to follow the directions on their own. Positive narration repeats your directions in a positive manner.

Some students may not be focused when you initially give your directions for an activity so they will have a hard time following them. Effective teachers recognize that by narrating on-task students, they give unfocused, off-task students a second chance to hear and see what they need to be doing. With positive narration, teachers can repeat their directions without nagging, pleading, or begging unfocused students. Narration provides these students with a model of success.

Consider the previous scenario with John Michael. John Michael isn't a mischievous student. He might have just been checked out for a few minutes. With positive narration, he now has the ability to get back on task. (And let's face it, from time to time we all check out for a bit or catch ourselves daydreaming, right?)

Positive narration demonstrates positive withitness. *Withitness* is a teacher's awareness of what is going on with all students at all times in the classroom. The education community identified *withitness* as a tool of highly effective teachers (Kounin, 1970), but research and training programs struggle to figure out ways to train teachers to increase it.

Positive narration, however, requires a teacher to scan the classroom for students who are following directions, helping him or her develop and employ withitness in a positive manner.

Gives Off-Task Students Informal Warnings Before They Receive Consequences

Even with the most precise directions, you are likely to have some students who choose to ignore your directions. These students hear positive narration as a warning to get on track, especially if you employ your strong teacher voice when narrating. This alerts them in a positive way before you move to a consequence.

Let's return to the student John Michael. Maybe he's one of those students who is easily distracted. Let's assume he heard your directions but decides that reorganizing his pencils is a better idea. Because positive narration increases your withitness, you quickly notice his off-task behavior while scanning the room to narrate. In order to support John Michael to make the right decision and begin writing silently in his journal, a No-Nonsense Nurturer will narrate students near him using a strong teacher voice. This provides an added reminder (or warning) for John Michael, and he will likely get back on task writing in his journal before you need to issue a consequence. (For more about consequences, see chapter 5, page 106.)

Respects Student Autonomy and Builds Self-Control

All too often, teachers rely on consequences as the primary step in addressing off-task behavior. This misstep may undermine students' efforts to build their sense of autonomy and self-control. When teachers use positive narration effectively, consistently, and equitably, students grow to recognize it as the way the teacher thoughtfully and respectfully offers support, encourages excellence, and extends opportunities for students to self-correct.

Gives Students a Chance to Regulate Their Own Behavior Before Receiving Consequences

When a student has the opportunity to reflect on his or her own choices and then make the decision to change those choices, that student is regulating his or her own behavior, which allows for independence, growth, and learning. Our goal as educators is for students to become independent adults. When you narrate appropriate behavior, students have the opportunity to practice important self-regulation skills.

Allows More Time for Students to Process Directions

If students' processing speeds require extra time to understand verbal directions, narration is a powerful technique for allowing this to occur without singling out a particular student or requiring additional attention from the teacher. Narration is a simple, neutral *noticing* of who is following a precise direction. Narration provides students requiring an accommodation for more processing time the extra time they need to follow the stated precise direction.

Recognizes Student Behavior Without the Shortcomings of Praise

As mentioned earlier, positive narration is an opportunity to notice students who immediately follow directions, but it should not be praise-based (Ferguson, 2013). Positive narration often tends to be misinterpreted as praise. Though both strategies can motivate and build relationships with students, there are significant differences between them. In short, positive narration is *not* praise.

When you praise students, you are making a judgment about their behavior. Here are some examples.

- ▸ "I like how Sophia is doing such a good job working quietly with her partner."
- ▸ "Elisha is doing an excellent job paying attention to me while I teach."

However, there are rarely recognized downsides to constantly praising students for following directions or for behaviors. Let's investigate.

Research asserts that students interpret frequent praise from teachers as an indicator that they are not doing well and, hence, need extra motivation (Dweck, 2007; Klei Borrero & Canter, 2018). They interpret praise for simply getting to work or paying attention as a clear message that teachers have low expectations for their behavior. Most teachers report that they eventually feel inauthentic when constantly repeating expressions such as "I like . . . ," "Great job!" or "Well done!" (Klei Borrero & Canter, 2018). Because praise is a judgment, it can make student behaviors more about the teacher than the student.

The following are examples of ineffective narration.

- ▸ "*I like* the way Andrea has gotten right to work."
- ▸ "*I love* the way Erin moved right to his seat."
- ▸ "Noah is doing a *great job* paying attention."

When students choose to do the right thing, the narration should focus on them, not the teacher's feelings about them.

Here are some effective positive narration examples.

- ▸ "*Andrea* has gotten right to work."
- ▸ "*Erin* has moved right to his seat."
- ▸ "*Noah* is tracking the speaker."

When narrating, No-Nonsense Nurturers focus on the students instead of themselves.

Many teachers use *I like* and *I love* because this is what they have heard or what they were trained to use; others just use these phrases without thinking. Take a minute to consider this. Do you want to lead with what the *student* does or with what *you* like or love? It is likely that by leading with the student's name, you are making a much more positive impression and strengthening your relationship with the student because you are noticing him or her, not the behavior you like or love.

Teachers who constantly praise students for doing what they expect, such as following directions, diminish the significance of the praise they give when students do something truly extraordinary or rigorous. Following a teacher's directions is simply not praiseworthy. Following directions is an expectation. Working hard to raise a grade on a test or persevering during a challenging task is praiseworthy!

No-Nonsense Nurturers save praise for students' academic resiliency, perseverance, grit, and achievement. Meaningful praise around these things, instead of behavior expectations, motivates students toward academic excellence and self-discipline.

The following are examples of appropriate praise.

▶ "Katy, I can see that you are really focusing on your topic sentences and supporting details. Keep it up!"

▶ "Tyler, it's great how much you have improved your reading scores. What is your key to success?"

▶ "Jamila, your persistence paid off. You brought your score up from 65 percent to 83 percent. Excellent work!"

Includes Descriptions

When you use positive narration, you are stating a simple, nonjudgmental description of the behavior you observe. This provides examples of success for students to follow, such as the following.

▶ "Sophia is working with her partner using her whisper voice."

▶ "Elisha is tracking me."

▶ "Evan is moving directly to his seat."

As No-Nonsense Nurturers, we should always look to our students to teach us and raise our levels of cultural awareness. Following is an example of how one of my students supported my understanding of the cultural implications of praise-based narration while I was a principal in East Palo Alto, California.

Demetrius came to our school in November of his kindergarten year. By this time, he had already been expelled from two kindergarten classes at other schools in the community. His mother came to me desperate. Understanding that Demetrius was challenging for many teachers, she didn't know what to do.

Demetrius's behaviors were aggressive, and he often hit other students or the teacher when he felt frustrated. He was intelligent but really struggled to express himself verbally and on paper. After better understanding his struggles, I decided to place him in the classroom of one of the No-Nonsense Nurturers Lee and I would eventually study. She had firm and clear expectations for her students but cared deeply for each and every one of them. I knew her structures and care would support a student who had needs Demetrius exhibited.

During the rest of his kindergarten year, Demetrius made progress but still struggled, as did the adults. His teacher, his mom, and I all worked tirelessly to support him and we remained consistent and vigilant—we all believed in Demetrius.

While Demetrius spent about half of his kindergarten career in the office or with a teacher's aide, he progressed and moved on to first grade where his successes started adding up because of the consistency the adults maintained and the positive structures that supported him. By second grade, he was only visiting my office with positive referrals. Our perseverance, as well as a consistently loving and firm approach, had paid off. Demetrius was performing in the top 25 percent of his class in both reading and mathematics, and his behaviors were rarely a concern anymore.

One day early in Demetrius's third-grade year, I was in the halls observing class transitions. He was proudly leading his line to technology class. He took his line leader position very seriously! Watching him, I had an overwhelming feeling of pride for how well he was doing. I also took pride in the adults who had helped him. We had done it. Demetrius was a successful young student.

Wanting to share this feeling with Demetrius, I noted as he and his class passed, "I love the way Demetrius is leading his class to technology! Great work!"

Without missing a beat, Demetrius stopped the line, turned around, and said, "Principal Klei, don't love me for leading my line the way I am supposed to, love me for being a strong black male who is working hard and getting good grades." As his words ended, he turned around and continued to lead his line to technology class.

continued →

I stood there stunned as he walked away. Frankly, it took me a few minutes to gather what *he was teaching me*. Demetrius was literally relaying the words and message that I had spoken to him so many times when he came to my office for his inappropriate actions. He didn't want me to praise him for his behaviors (leading the line silently), he wanted me to praise him for being an intelligent, hardworking student! Demetrius was teaching me the ultimate lesson of *praise versus narration*.

That afternoon, I shared the story of what Demetrius had taught me with the staff. I should note that everyone knew Demetrius, because teachers in other grade levels would often try to support him on their breaks during his first few years with us. The teachers shared in my pride in his accomplishment, but the lesson he taught me also resonated with them. We needed to use our praise for our students' perseverance of academic pursuits and achievements. Behaviors aren't praiseworthy, they are expectations. If we praise students for expectations, it inadvertently communicates low expectations and none of us want that. What Demetrius taught us was a gift. Thus, narration changed at our school and remained positive but *not* praise-based.

How Positive Narration Supports Student Behavior

This section explores how No-Nonsense Nurturers use positive narration to support student behaviors. Do the following to effectively employ positive narration.

- After giving directions, immediately scan the room to monitor students' behavior (to test or increase your withitness). Look for students who are on task, especially those you find challenging.

- Quickly narrate on-task students. *Within two seconds* of completing your directions, begin positively narrating students who are following your directions. Waiting too long gives students the opportunity to get off task.

- Make a three-part statement. If you work with elementary students, use the following formula.

    a. Student's name: Jim

    b. Verb: *Is*

    c. Behavior: Silently writing in his journal

If you work with middle or secondary school students (who do not want to be singled out), you may choose to group students like the following.

    a. Name of student's group: Row two, table four, Cassie's table

    b. Verb: *Is* or *are*

    c. Behavior: Using their library voices and solving problem number two

Narrate about two or three students, including one you find challenging. Narrating the behavior of two or three students will accomplish the following.

- Repeating your directions will ensure everyone understands them.

- Clearly communicating to all students will demonstrate you are on top of behaviors in the classroom.

Don't overnarrate. Narrating about two or three students is enough. When you start narrating more than two or three times, your narration loses its effectiveness. When scanning the class for students to narrate, always check if the students you find challenging are on task. If so, choose at least one to narrate. By *challenging*, I mean students who are frequently off task, disruptive, or possibly defiant. It is up to teachers to break this cycle and help these students find success. Positive narration (focusing on what students are doing well versus highlighting what they are struggling with) can assist with this.

In addition, any students whom teachers find challenging often just need more attention than their peers. By narrating for them, you are calling positive attention to their successful actions. This often prevents them from causing a disruption in order to get the negative attention the system has taught them to seek.

When students know you are monitoring and holding them to 100 percent on-task expectation, they are much more likely to choose to be and remain on task. The more positive feedback you give to them, the more you motivate them to strive for success in your classroom.

Typically, you will use a strong teacher voice when narrating. You want to be sure all students can clearly hear you as you identify those who are following directions. This confirms for students that you are noticing whether they are on task. Using a strong teacher voice while narrating communicates that your high expectations are a priority and you are aware when those expectations are met. Following are some strategies for making narrations most effective in your classroom.

Narrate Before You Give Consequences to Off-Task Students

As previously noted, less-effective teachers tend to immediately respond to off-task students and create a negative tone and momentum in their classrooms (Klei Borrero & Canter, 2018). Avoid this temptation because although it may come from a good place and you want to engage all students, it sets a negative tone in your classroom and inhibits your ability to build relationships with students you find challenging. Instead, use positive narration about on-task students *before* you attempt to provide consequences for off-task or disruptive students. It only takes a few seconds and can motivate many students to choose to follow your directions, sometimes eliminating the need for a consequence.

Teachers often wonder about the effectiveness of narration during independent, silent work time or if narration can be distracting to students. However, students consistently report that narration isn't disruptive (Klei Borrero & Canter, 2018). For those deep in thought or engaged in their learning, narration becomes white noise. Students who might be struggling or in need of a boost often hear narration as a welcome reminder as to what they should be doing or to get back on track with their learning. If your class is working silently, but one or two students are off task, just lower your voice for the narration. The narration will support the one or two students who need it without distracting others.

Narrate Every Sixty Seconds During Instruction

In addition to motivating students to follow your directions and *get* on task, positive narration motivates students to *stay* on task during instructional activities.

At the beginning of the year or when re-norming your classroom expectations, narrate approximately once every sixty seconds during instructional activities. Scan your class and positively narrate two students who are staying on task and engaged with their assignment. This sends a clear message that you expect students to stay engaged. Narrating every sixty seconds or so helps your class build their momentum and stamina on instructional activities, and once they reach the goal, you can decrease significantly or eliminate narration altogether. However, if you find students are becoming disengaged, narrate before you provide consequences.

Narrate Two Students Before and After Working With Students Individually or in Small Groups

Teachers often take time to work with students individually or in small groups. Throughout the year as you do this, consider narrating two students who are actively engaged in their work before turning your attention to the one student or small group. As you work with small groups, your withitness decreases considerably because your attention is on their learning. However, you can set up the entire class for success by narrating before and after engaging with an individual student or small groups, looking up every minute or two to monitor (and narrate, if needed). Then, as soon as you finish the discussion or teachable moment, narrate two more students to ensure continued engaged momentum in your classroom. By narrating during these times, you communicate a high level of care, and students realize you are still monitoring their progress and engagement.

Narrate Throughout Transitions

When students are moving from one location to another, the likelihood of off-task behavior dramatically increases. To prevent this and allow for quicker transitions, positively narrate throughout your transitions. Here are some examples.

- ▸ "Evan is moving quickly and safely to the next lab station."
- ▸ "Sara and Holly are maintaining level-one voices."
- ▸ "Kareem's group is already reading directions for the second station."

Beware of vague positive narrations such as, "Kelsey has gotten right to work." A student who needs support may not know what *right to work* means. Instead narrate, "Kelsey is working silently on her journal." This supports every student in the room and points out exactly what Kelsey is doing to be successful.

Follow the 3:1 Rule of Teacher-Student Interaction

No-Nonsense Nurturers have learned that a key to creating life-altering relationships with students is the frequency of authentic, positive interactions they have with them. These teachers live by the *3:1 rule*, which means they take great pains to make *three times* as many positive comments to students as negative ones. For example, if these teachers provide a consequence to a student for being off task, they find three opportunities to narrate the student when he or she is on task as soon as possible.

Phase Out or Modify Positive Narration as You Establish a No-Nonsense Nurturing Culture

As the school year progresses, you will build stronger relationships and have solid policies, procedures, and routines in place. At that point, the need for positive narration will decrease. However, you may consider using narration in the following situations.

- After sets of new directions or directions you give later in the day, when students tend to be more tired and distracted

- Every two or three minutes during instructional activities

- During transitions

- When you notice students starting to get off task

- When supporting student use of academic concepts, like the following examples (I refer to the following as *academic narration*)

    ▷ "Wanda used the Pythagorean theorem to solve problem three."

    ▷ "Richard's group is using a graphic organizer to note its evidence from the lab."

    ▷ "Nataki is editing her conclusion statement."

  This supports students with academic strategies they may not have considered while working independently or in their groups.

As students master classroom expectations, you can reduce the frequency of narration even further; however, you should also reflect on the following.

- Consider keeping a high frequency of positive narration during transitions. These are much more difficult times for teachers to keep students on task, and narration tends to make transitions much faster.

- If you are providing consequences to more students than usual for disruptive or off-task behavior, try to increase the frequency of positive narration.

- Be sure to increase the frequency of positive narration before and after a school break, such as a holiday or vacation. Students tend to need more structure during these times, and precise directions and positive narration, used in a proactive fashion, will significantly decrease off-task behaviors.

- If you have some students you find especially challenging, positively narrate their behavior throughout the year.

Differentiating between elementary and secondary students is also important when delivering positive narration. It is effective to narrate groups at the secondary level (identifying the group, for example, by rows, sides of the room, grade levels, as well as by group name). It is important to note that not all secondary students want their name said out loud or attached to an affirmation. It is your responsibility to establish a relationship with your students to find out how they would like to be recognized through narration. However, the high school teachers we studied reported that positive narration significantly impacts high school classroom cultures and student engagement, so don't leave out this important step. All students, no matter what their age, need to be recognized and affirmed (Klei Borrero & Canter, 2018).

Positive Narration for Students With Additional Needs

While positive narration works for most students, it is important to notice how students with additional needs react to narration. Students with identified needs might feel the teacher only points them out for their missteps or when their actions need support or redirection. Since positive narration notices students for following directions and supports them with a positive reminder of what the directions are, most students with additional needs react positively to narration, especially once they understand its purpose. In addition, positive narration is a support for students who struggle with processing. Narration repeats directions in a way to keep these students on track and gives them additional chances to hear and see the expectation.

However, there is a chance that a small percentage of students, particularly those with 504 plans or IEPs, will react negatively to narration. If this happens, ask yourself the following.

▶ "Are these student acting in a negative manner because they think they might be in trouble? Do I need to explain the meaning of positive narration?"

▶ "Is this student unable to accept being noticed in a positive light, especially by me? Is there something missing in our relationship?"

If you are confident that students understand the purpose of narration and still cannot accept being noticed through positive narration, then you may need to find other ways to privately recognize them. You might give a nonverbal cue such as a thumbs-up or a wink, place a sticky note with a confirming phrase on a student's desk, or quietly narrate the student so only he or she can hear it, all with a goal of strengthening your relationship and letting them know they are on the right track.

Conclusion

In this chapter, you learned how to use positive narration to reinforce precise directions in a neutral, affirming tone. Positive narration allows students to hear your directions in an encouraging fashion so they can self-correct and monitor their own behaviors. Because narration recognizes students in a positive light, it is an early relationship builder in your classroom. With a little practice, positive narration will become an effortless and productive part of your daily routine. Narration puts you and your students in a positive mood, ready to handle the challenges of rigorous learning opportunities.

The next chapter presents step 3 in the No-Nonsense Nurturer four-step model—implement accountability systems—and how precise directions, positive narration, and student relationships relate to and support these systems.

Video

This brief video montage was designed for readers to view the steps of the No-Nonsense Nurturer four-step model individually and in teams. Scan this code to view No-Nonsense Nurturers as they demonstrate positive narration in action.

Positive Narration in Action

www.ct3education.com/book/positive-narration

Reflection Activities

The reflection activities on pages 101–104 are designed to help you reflect on your current professional practice and support your journey to becoming a No-Nonsense Nurturer. You may choose to complete them individually or in teams.

Keep a Positive Narration Journal

Positive narration is one of the key features to building relationships with your students and setting positive, high expectations in your classroom from minute one, day one of the school year.

Take several minutes to reflect on and answer the following questions.

What resonates with you about positive narration?

How and when do you plan to use positive narration?

Do you plan to teach your students why you use positive narration? If so, how will you introduce it?

What makes you nervous or causes you to pause about adding positive narration to your practice?

Use a Positive Narration Log

After you give precise directions, scan for compliance rather than defiance, and use positive narration. Notice how positive narration is strengthening your relationships with specific students. Log your observations in the following chart.

Student name	How did the student respond to positive narration?	Are any adjustments needed? If so, what?	How is this building a better relationship?

Continue Your Journal

After a few days of using positive narration, answer the following questions.

How are you finding that positive narration reinforces your directions?

How is the tone in your classroom different after introducing narration?

How has positive narration impacted off-task behavior?

Which students is positive narration working for? Are there students it isn't working for?

Are you experiencing any struggles with positive narration? If so, how might you make adjustments?

Practice Positive Narration

Positive narration is a powerful strategy but not intuitive for many teachers. As the teacher, you need to practice, practice, practice, so it becomes second nature.

Review the precise directions in the following chart. Then, challenge yourself to write two or three positive narrations for each set of directions. Use a student's name for each narration. After completing the table, in your strong teacher voice, practice with a colleague or in front of the mirror, giving the precise direction and then immediately starting positive narration.

Directions	Three Positive Narration Statements
"Silently walk to your seat and begin the Do Now."	
"Work with your partner at level-one volume to complete your fluency check. Chart your results at your station."	
"When I say *go*, move to your next lab station and begin working on the activity card with your group using level-one voices. You have seven minutes to complete this station. Go!"	

If you aren't sure if you are narrating effectively, try this: record yourself on video for fifteen minutes and count your positive versus negative statements. If you don't have video access, invite a colleague, coach, or administrator to come in for a few minutes and keep a tally for you. Use the data you collect to set your next goal for fine-tuning and expanding your use of positive narration. Remember, your goal is to make at least three positive comments for every redirection or consequence.

CHAPTER 5

Implement Accountability Systems

In the previous chapters, you learned about precise directions and positive narration to support students on the path to success in your classroom and as some of the stepping stones to building strong relationships with students. In this chapter, we will look at accountability systems. See figure 5.1.

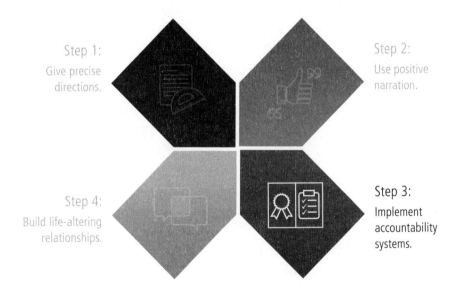

Figure 5.1: Implement accountability systems.

Accountability systems are composed of consequences (for off-task or negative behaviors) and incentives (for on-task or positive behaviors). This chapter investigates stay-in-the-game and restorative conversations, documentation for consequences and incentives, supportive strategies for behaviors you may find challenging, guidelines for giving consequences and incentives, and finally, consequences and incentives for students with additional needs. It explores how accountability systems can continue to support relationships, learning, and a positive culture in your classroom at even higher levels.

However, before discussing accountability systems, it is important to describe the differences between *punishment* and *consequences*. Remember, the cornerstone of No-Nonsense Nurturers' work are the relationships they build with students. They see the good in students and look at every opportunity as one to learn and grow.

Punishment Versus Consequences

The Merriam-Webster Dictionary defines *punishment* (n.d.) as "suffering, pain, or loss that serves as retribution," while it defines *consequence* (n.d.) as "a conclusion derived though logic." Take a minute and consider these definitions. *Punishment* has a very negative connotation, while *consequence* has a more positive one.

There is no place in a No-Nonsense Nurturer's classroom for punishment. Students do not learn from public shaming or being made to feel like they don't belong. It is inevitable; you and your students will make mistakes and experience failure. There are often consequences for these mistakes, but that doesn't mean they must all be negative. They need to be learning opportunities! Table 5.1 examines the differences between punishment and consequences.

Table 5.1: Punishment Versus Consequences

	Punishment	Consequence
Purpose	To penalize for an offense, regulate and control, inflict shame	To redirect behaviors, build self-regulation and self-control
Attitude of adult	Hostility, exasperation, disappointment	Love, care, concern
Social-emotional impact on a child	Feelings of fear, guilt, rejection, marginalization or exclusion (disempowering)	Feelings of security, care, membership (empowering)
Emphasis and expression	Emphasis on individual, judgmental expression delivered out of anger or frustration, aggressive tone	Emphasis on behavior, objective, nonjudgmental response, calming tone
Message	"You need to change." "I am in control." "I don't have time for this." "I don't have patience for you."	"Different choices will help you." "You can choose to control yourself." "Because I care about you . . ." "You are worth it."
Outcome	Punishment is often unexpected, unpredictable, arbitrary, grows "harsher" with each step	Consequences are expected, predictable, logical, investment increases for both student and teacher with each step

Source: R. Frank, personal communication, March 16, 2018.

Accountability systems are important to ensure and deepen relationships with all your students. When presented with care and support, consequences communicate to students that you care too much about them to let them fail or make poor choices (Klei Borrero & Canter, 2018; Responsive Classroom, 2011). Let's examine some of the benefits of using consequences as part of your accountability system.

Creates a Culture of High Expectations

After you give directions and narrate, students typically engage in academically rigorously work. How they work, independently or with one another, determines how you will engage in accountability systems in your classroom. If students don't make the proper choices, providing a consequence can demonstrate that you hold every student in your classroom to high expectations because you care.

While working as a teacher in Phoenix, Arizona, I was reminded of the importance of providing consequences.

Ms. Likely was a second-year corps member for Teach for America. She was a teacher with a lot of will to improve her practice, working long days and on weekends to prepare her lessons to support student learning. She spent time tutoring students, providing extra support and building relationships with them. She gave precise directions and did a pretty good job with narration. Ms. Likely had an incentive system tied to clear behavioral and learning objectives, but she was afraid of consequences. She had a mindset that if she gave consequences to students for their poor choices, they would not like her.

Through some coaching, I challenged her mindset. I asked why she thought her parents gave her consequences when she was younger and didn't come home at the set curfew or when she argued with her siblings. Her answers were thoughtful and, in the end, she noted that her parents created guidelines while raising her because they loved her and wanted her to make good choices as an adult. Her parents set a high bar for her to meet, and they cared too much about her to let her make poor choices.

I continued to push her. I asked, "If your parents had consequences and that demonstrated high expectations and love to you, why are you afraid of holding your students to high expectations and demonstrating to them that you care too much about them to let them make poor choices?"

continued →

A lightbulb began to go off for Ms. Likely, so I continued to push. "Do you think it was important to your parents that you liked them or that you respected them and what they had to do to train and support you to become a productive member of society?" She smiled and noted, "My mom always told me, 'I am not here to be your friend, I am here to be your mother and that is a job I will not fail.'"

There it was. Ms. Likely was beginning to understand that consequences were not about punishment but setting high expectations in her classroom and beyond, just as her parents had done for her.

Supports a Safe and Supportive Classroom Culture

In order for students to fully engage in learning, they need to feel safe and supported in your classroom. It is only when students feel safe that they take academic risks and explore their learning, independently or with their peers. When well executed, consequences don't demonstrate anger or punishment to students; they communicate that you will catch them when they fall. If their peers are creating an environment that is not conducive to learning, you will work to get the environment safe and back on track. In safe and supportive classrooms, students take academic risks with the teacher and one another, which creates opportunities for students to engage in rigorous academic discourse and support one another's learning (National Center on Safe and Supportive Learning Environments, 2018).

Helps Students Self-Regulate Their Behavior

One of our goals as educators is to support students and guide them to becoming highly productive citizens. Learning to self-regulate, make strong choices, and monitor their behaviors is something we need to support all learners to do, no matter where they are in their academic careers. Accountability systems support students individually and how they work within larger groups. Clear, consistent expectations and consequences support students to hold themselves accountable as they leave school and enter the workforce. In addition, learning to hold others accountable is an essential skill as students navigate post-secondary education and the workplace. Self-regulating is a life skill that, when executed well, helps students learn valuable lessons.

Supports Teacher-Student Relationships

When well executed, consequences ensure fairness and consistency (Duncan-Andrade, 2007; Klei Borrero & Canter, 2018). They help teachers regulate and support all behaviors and expectations for many students at one time. When teachers demonstrate to students that they can manage the learning environment, they earn the respect of their students and further deepen the relationships they have with every learner. As educators, we are charged with supporting sometimes hundreds of students every day. It's important to have systems in place to help us build relationships with students and ensure that the environment is safe and fair, allowing for cooperative and collaborative learning environments.

Strategies for Presenting Consequences

Life is full of logical consequences, and No-Nonsense Nurturers hold their students accountable for following directions and staying engaged in learning opportunities because it is important for all students to learn. During our research, many teachers reported being afraid to give consequences because they perceive them as negative instead of as a way to support student success (Klei Borrero & Canter, 2018). For No-Nonsense Nurturers, consequences are not about punishment; consequences are about teachers showing students they care too much to let them fail in any classroom activity or task. Consequences are ways to hold students and teachers accountable. Failure happens. In fact, we learn the most from our failures, and they provide us with the greatest opportunities to grow and build stronger relationships with students.

In order to establish a classroom culture that promotes academic success, it's essential that teachers communicate with a consistent tone of high expectations for all students, especially those who choose to be off task or disruptive. Setting high, supportive expectations with consistent, fair consequences for students who do not follow precise directions or meet rigorous expectations sets a tone of rigor and care in the classroom. Consequences should communicate, "I care too much about you to let you fail," versus "I am angry with you; therefore, I am punishing you." High expectations and consistent, predictable consequences support your relationships with all students (Asch, 2010; Ferguson, 2008; Marzano, 2010; Ware, 2006). When done well, consequences are opportunities to demonstrate high levels of care for your students.

No-Nonsense Nurturers know students will test them, especially at the beginning of the year. Why? Because they are children, and they are naturally programmed to try to get their way. But No-Nonsense Nurturers have learned effective ways to provide consequences that support the learning environment for all students.

It is important to note that although most students make a *choice* to follow or not to follow directions, you may have some who aren't making a choice but rather struggling because of a special need. For those students, be sure to follow their 504 plans or IEPs and determine the best way to provide directions and consequences accordingly. If a 504 plan or an IEP doesn't exist, then consider the following.

▸ Do you believe this student really isn't making a choice but instead is struggling or dealing with some kind of issue? How can you advocate for specialized testing or support services?

▸ Are you sure the student cannot learn from the consequence, or are you making that assumption? Can you work with this student to make sure he or she realizes consequences are learning opportunities to promote success in your classroom? Often, until a teacher implements clear and precise directions followed with positive narration, a student doesn't understand when a consequence is coming and, therefore, reacts negatively. Once a teacher executes the first two steps of the four-step model effectively, most students understand the *why* and *when* of consequences, take note of the warnings, and adjust their behaviors and choices appropriately.

If you believe the student has the capability to regulate his or her own behavior but needs additional support with consequences, continue with the following steps while working on your relationship with the student.

Respond to Disruptive and Off-Task Behavior Within Ten to Twenty Seconds

You have approximately ten to twenty seconds after stating precise directions and completing positive narrations before providing consequences to students who have chosen not to follow directions (Bondy et al., 2007). It is important to note that the longer you wait to redirect students, the higher the probability that more students will join the off-task or disruptive behaviors (Canter, 2010; Kounin, 1970).

Provide Consequences From Your Accountability Hierarchy

No-Nonsense Nurturers establish a hierarchy of consequences to communicate a sense of fairness and consistency. An *accountability hierarchy* starts with a minimal consequence, such as a warning. If a student continues to disrupt, the consequences (and accountability) become progressively more significant for the student and the teacher.

You can develop accountability hierarchies in a variety of ways. Many schools establish these for you; others do not. Some teachers choose to create hierarchies with their students on the first day of school, while others simply teach the hierarchies they have developed. Regardless of how you create your hierarchy, it is important to check with your administration for approval. It is also pivotal to explicitly teach it to your students. Your accountability hierarchy should not surprise students, and you should execute it with consistency and fairness.

Teach students why you have a hierarchy, when you will use it, and how to appropriately react to a consequence. Explain that consequences in your classroom are to keep students on track because their education is important to you and you are there to support them through mistakes and successes. Thus, you must hold them accountable. This learning opportunity should build relationships and trust with all students while setting high expectations.

Figure 5.2 and figure 5.3 (page 112) show sample accountability hierarchies that you can adjust to meet your and your students' needs. Be sure the hierarchy notes how you will hold both yourself and students accountable. Remember, if consequences are opportunities to build relationships and trust, you have to engage in the work.

Consequence	Student Accountability	Teacher Accountability
First	Verbal warning	Track (on clipboard or electronic device)
Second	Focus spot	Track; speak with student about change of venue to support his or her learning
Third	Five-minute reflection (likely during recess or center time, perhaps in the focus spot)	Track; stay-in-the-game conversation
Fourth	Complete reflection sheet; students should note on reflection sheet distracting behaviors from the day and how and why it is important to remain on track Student notes anything bothering him or her or how the teacher can provide support	Track; discussion with student based on reflection sheet Call to family member to discuss disruptions and plan to get student back on track
Fifth (or serious disruption)	Visit to administrator to reset	Track; restorative conversation with student before he or she returns to class

Figure 5.2: Sample grades K–5 accountability hierarchy (self-contained classroom).

*Visit **go.SolutionTree.com/behavior** for a free reproducible version of this figure.*

Consequence	Student Accountability	Teacher accountability
First	Verbal warning	Track (on clipboard or electronic device)
Second	Teacher proximity, seat change, or Last One Out	Track; stay-in-the-game conversation focusing the need to follow precise directions
Third (or serious disruption)	Visit to administrator to reset	Track; restorative conversation; call to family member

Figure 5.3: Sample middle or secondary school accountability hierarchy (for 50- to 180-minute class periods).

*Visit **go.SolutionTree.com/behavior** for a free reproducible version of this figure.*

These accountability hierarchies refer to stay-in-the-game conversations and restorative conversations. Stay-in-the-game and restorative conversations have a similar purpose—to let students know their chosen behaviors are not in their best interest, but you believe in them, and they can change their behaviors. However, the time it takes to have these conversations and the amount of student voice in these conversations differ. These kinds of conversations should be an essential part of your accountability system. They let students know you are paying attention, you expect them to be accountable for their actions, and most important, you care about their success in the classroom.

Stay-in-the-Game Conversations

Stay-in-the-game conversations are quick ten- to thirty-second reminders to students. While you will likely check in with students to make sure nothing is wrong or out of the ordinary, it is more of a teacher-directed conversation, noting the teacher's belief in the student and a helpful hint for getting back on track. The following is the basic four-step formula for stay-in-the-game conversations.

1. Restate on- or off-task behaviors.

2. Redirect for desired behavior and restate precise directions.

3. Encourage the student.

4. Extend support if needed.

Restorative Conversations

Restorative conversations are lengthier conversations and must always happen if you need to remove a student from your classroom. While you address the distracting behaviors, the student's voice in these conversations is incredibly important. The student can describe why he or she is struggling and note possible supports that might help him or her in class. Through restorative conversations, teachers can often build deeper relationships with students because they learn of accommodations students might need or challenges they are facing—at school or at home. Through these conversations, you have a chance to truly listen to students, humanize their experiences, and if applicable, share stories of how you relate to their struggles, thus humanizing yourself in their eyes.

For most of us, there are few aspects of teaching that are more stressful than dealing with students who continually choose to disrupt class, defy authority, or simply check out. It is a natural inclination for most teachers to take this behavior personally and distance themselves psychologically from these students. This inclination only makes a negative situation worse.

No-Nonsense Nurturers recognize the important message that a student's defiance holds for the teacher. If a student is so disruptive that he or she must be removed from the classroom, this is a clear sign that you need to immediately begin working on restoring and rebuilding your relationship.

Before any student, and especially a student you find challenging, returns to your class, talk with him or her either face-to-face (or by phone, if necessary). A restorative conversation allows you to identify how to better help the student succeed in your classroom. Make sure the student knows he or she is welcome back to class, but that you will not tolerate further disruptive behaviors because you care about his or her success. Give the student a chance to say what is bothering him or her and, if appropriate, ask if you can help the situation in any way. The following is the basic five-step formula for restorative conversations.

1. Restate the on- and off-task behaviors the student exhibited.

2. Redirect for desired behavior.

3. Listen to the student's perspective and needs.

4. Inquire or extend support to the student.

5. Provide encouragement and reintroduce the student to the classroom.

The following is an example of a restorative conversation between a high school English teacher and one of her seniors.

Ms. Gore: "Hey."

Talia: "Hi."

Ms. Gore: "So, what happened today?"

(Ms. Gore wants to make sure Talia feels heard and that they come to a resolution they both can agree on. She begins with listening to the student's perspective.)

Talia: "I mean, the lesson is just boring. And I failed my precalculus test. So, I was irritated."

Ms. Gore: "So, you were irritated and bored. You failed your precalculus assessment?"

Talia: "Yes."

Ms. Gore: "Oh, I'm sorry. I know you were putting some work into your mathematics class. Yeah, I hear that the lesson was boring. I was actually feeling a little bored teaching it. I try to make things interesting, but sometimes, some days, I miss the mark and I see you guys getting bored. Is there anything else going on that I should know about? Because that's not like you. What happened today?"

Talia: "No. I mean, I am a senior, Ms. Gore."

Ms. Gore: "Uh-huh."

Talia: "I have a lot going on—finals and college applications—I am just, I am tired."

Ms. Gore: "Yeah, sounds like you are stressed."

Talia: "Yeah, I am."

Ms. Gore: "Obviously, I need you to engage in the way I know you can. Even if the class is getting a little boring. You know, you can always talk to me after class, but the way you handled your frustration today, with that outburst, was unacceptable, Talia. What can you do differently next time?"

(Ms. Gore notes the behavior that needs to change and redirects the student to the appropriate behavior in the future.)

Talia: "Instead of talking back to you when you redirect me, I could just listen and deal with the lesson."

Ms. Gore: "Uh-huh. Is there anything I could differently that would make it easier for you to react like that?"

(Ms. Gore extends additional support.)

Talia: "I mean, it wasn't you. It was me. You didn't do anything. You did what you, as a teacher, you were supposed to do."

Ms. Gore: "Well, if there is something I am doing that you want me to do differently, you can always say that. You shouldn't necessarily blurt it out in the middle of class, but I am always open to hearing what I can do to be more helpful with my class or with your stress level. Got it?"

Talia: "Yeah, got it."

Ms. Gore: "OK, great. Is there support I can provide with those college applications?"

Talia: "I don't know. Thanks for asking. I have an appointment with my counselor on Wednesday. Maybe then I will feel better about them."

Ms. Gore: "Well, I hope your day gets better; thanks for coming in. I'm looking forward to having you back in class tomorrow. And be sure to check in with me if there is anything I can do to support you with those applications."

(Ms. Gore makes sure Talia knows she is welcome in the class tomorrow and she is available for support with Talia's stressors.)

Talia: "Thanks. I will, Ms. Gore."

Detentions are often found on accountability hierarchies. If you choose to use detention, consider the outcome you are trying to accomplish. The point of detention should be for the teacher to re-establish trust and respect with the student. Thus, No-Nonsense Nurturers do not send a student to detention; rather, they hold detention in their own classrooms so they can meet with the student to note what needs to change and how they can support that student in their classroom.

An alternative that many No-Nonsense Nurturers prefer to detention is something we call *last one out*. This strategy involves keeping the student after class for a short time to reset his or her behavior for the next day. This activity includes having a quick stay-in-the-game conversation with the student before the next period. It gives the teacher and student a chance to discuss the behavior that needs to change; it also gives the student a chance to share his or her thoughts or feelings.

When suggesting this type of strategy with middle and high school teachers, I often hear concerns about students being late to their next class. Although students being late to their next class is a legitimate concern with this strategy, try using a staff meeting to note solutions to making it work in your school. Typically, teachers can keep a student for less than two minutes, have a quick stay-in-the-game conversation, and the student can still make it to the next class on time.

Last one out is an easy, immediate consequence that keeps the responsibility of consequences with you and allows you to build relationships with students. Although there may be some logistical challenges in executing this strategy, think creatively with colleagues and find a way to make it work in your school.

Provide a Quick, Firm, Yet Respectful Redirect (Verbal Warning)

When you observe students choosing to receive a consequence, verbally redirect their behavior using the following simple formula.

- **Student's name:** Michael
- **Behavior desired:** "The directions are to work silently."
- **Consequence:** "This is your one warning for today."
- **Affirm:** "You are capable. Get started."

Let the student know that he or she has received his or her only warning, and be sure to record the warning on a clipboard or phone app. While you might have intentions of remembering consequences, you have far more important things to think about, and the consistency of your consequences is imperative to a successful classroom culture. Physically documenting the consequence also communicates to students that you care about their success and consistency is important in establishing a fair and just classroom culture.

Please note that some students interpret public accountability or discipline charts as public shaming. No-Nonsense Nurturers shy away from discipline charts and bulletin boards and keep consequence tracking more discreet on clipboards or smartphone applications.

Give Additional Consequences as Needed

When you observe students who continue to be off task or disruptive after receiving a verbal warning, remain calm, quick, firm, and respectful. Move to the next step in your accountability hierarchy, as in the following example.

- **Student's name:** Ethan
- **Behavior desired:** "The expectation is that you are silently working on your journal entry."
- **Consequence:** "This is the second time today I have had to speak to you about not following directions. You have chosen the second consequence in our accountability hierarchy, and during part of your

recess, we will have a conversation to make sure you are on track for the rest of the day."

▸ **Affirm:** "Get started on your work now. I know you can do this."

Let the student know that he or she has *chosen* to receive a consequence by engaging in inappropriate behavior or not following your precise directions. This communicates to students that they are responsible and accountable for their choices and the consequences they receive. It sends the message that you care too much for them not to be successful and are not simply picking on them (Farr, 2010).

As with a verbal warning, it is important to mark each consequence on a behavior tracker on your clipboard or phone app. Keeping track of consequences helps to maintain consistency. It communicates to students that you care too much about them to allow them to disrupt their learning time.

Please note: *The less you say, the more effective you will sound when providing a consequence.* Teachers who are nervous and unsure tend to ramble when providing consequences to students (Klei Borrero & Canter, 2018). No-Nonsense Nurturers use an economy of language to make their point without demeaning students, thereby demonstrating that they are able to manage the classroom and provide a productive learning environment.

Use as Strong a Teacher Voice as Needed

When issuing a consequence to students, it's important to speak in a no-nonsense tone that communicates to off-task students and their classmates that you mean business (Bondy & Ross, 2008; Brown, 2004). Your tone must be assertive enough to get into the hearing of the student you are redirecting, but never raise your voice. With some students, you may have to speak in a stronger tone than with others; however, you should never exhibit loss of control by yelling at a student. Yelling is punitive. A strong tone communicates high expectations and caring.

Be Aware of Your Body Language

What your body says when you deliver a message is as important as what you say (Jones, 2000). When providing a consequence, note the following.

▸ **Pause before you speak:** If you are walking around while providing
  a consequence to a student, you are not communicating that you
  take his or her behavior seriously. Stop what you are doing *before* you
  provide a consequence; the student deserves your attention for that
  brief moment.

▸ **Face the student:** Turn and directly face the student. Stand up straight or, if appropriate, lean in toward the student if he or she is close to you. Let your body language communicate that you are serious and care about how the student uses his or her academic learning time.

▸ **Make eye contact:** Look right into the eyes of the student you are redirecting. When you call out the student's name, he or she will most likely look at you, so it will be easy to make eye contact. A direct gaze increases the impact of your verbal message, and you can communicate high expectations and caring with your gaze.

Please also note that you need to know students' cultural norms. In some cultures, students will, out of deference (not defiance), avoid making eye contact. Allow them to do this and avoid comments like, "Look at me," because these comments communicate anger rather than compassion.

▸ **Get as close as is convenient and appropriate:** If possible, get in close proximity to the student you are redirecting. However, if you are in the middle of teaching a lesson or working one-to-one with another student, do not stop and take the time to walk over to the student causing a disruption. Making the redirection from where you are standing is more efficient, and it communicates to all students that you hold high academic and behavioral expectations for everyone.

Some teachers feel it is disrespectful to note a consequence to a student in front of his or her peers. Consider two things as you reflect on this.

1. **When issuing consequences out loud, No-Nonsense Nurturers are calling attention to the student's misbehavior, *not* the student:** The student's off-task behavior has called attention to him or her already. Issuing a consequence from the accountability hierarchy communicates to both the student and the rest of the class that you are creating a safe and respectful learning environment for everyone. For example:

    ▹ **Student's name**—Joy

    ▹ **Behavior desired**—"The precise direction is track me or your notes as I am teaching."

> ▷ **Consequence**—"This is the third time I have had to speak to you today. I will see you briefly after class so we can reset."

> ▷ **Affirm**—"You've got this. Keep up with your guided notes."

2. **Taking time to walk up to the student who is off task can be more distracting to the student and the class:** Consider the following scenario. You are teaching a lesson from the front of the class. Joy is off task in the second-to-last row. You take time to walk up to her, give a verbal redirection, and then head back to the board. Not only does this waste instructional time, but the whole class watches your actions. Joy likely feels embarrassed and singled out.

   Instead, after positively narrating about two or three students, provide a consequence from your accountability hierarchy to Joy from your position in front of the room, while making eye contact with her. Then, immediately follow up that consequence with a positive narration or two to take the focus off Joy. These actions will reduce the chance of a negative response from her and end the consequence on a positive note for the whole class. This is much more humanizing and communicates a higher level of care for Joy and the class. For example:

Narrate two to three students.

> ▷ "Paul is writing in his guided notes."

> ▷ "Katie is silently tracking the board, ready to move on."

You notice Joy talking to her neighbor. Provide a consequence.

> ▷ **Student's name**—Joy

> ▷ **Behavior desired**—"The precise direction is to silently track me or your notes as I am teaching."

> ▷ **Consequence**—"This is the third time I have had to speak to you today. I will see you briefly after class so we can reset with a stay-in-the-game conversation."

> ▷ **Affirm**—"You've got this. Keep up with your guided notes."

Narrate one or two students to take their attention off Joy and put it back on the lesson.

> ▷ "Daniel is tracking the board, ready to move on. Devante is silently completing his notes."

A mantra for No-Nonsense Nurturers is that *they expect 100 percent of their students to follow their directions 100 percent of the time.* But the 100 percent stance is all about *purpose, not power.* No-Nonsense Nurturers feel they need to demonstrate a low tolerance for inappropriate behavior to better help their students reach their full potential, not because these teachers are on a power trip.

Realistically, if you're going to be consistent in redirecting all off-task behavior, you need to sweat the small stuff. You *will* need to provide consequences to students who are engaging in what most teachers consider small problems. Most important, you will need to address inappropriate talking.

Remember, inappropriate or off-topic talking accounts for up to 80 percent of students' off-task behavior (Canter, 2010; Erdogan et al., 2010; Jones, 2000). In addition, inappropriate talking is often referred to as a *cornerstone behavior* (Canter, 2010). It is typically the first behavior students engage in to test your expectations of them.

If students see that you are not taking the small stuff seriously, there is a much greater chance they will test your resolve by getting more disruptive, perhaps by getting out of their seats, refusing to complete assignments, or eventually talking back and becoming defiant. Setting high expectations is a 24-7 job, and No-Nonsense Nurturers take it seriously.

Note that you must distinguish between students who are off task or disruptive due to a lack of understanding your directions and expectations versus those who are choosing to ignore your precise directions. If students lack understanding, you have a responsibility to practice how to behave appropriately with them. Reteach the expectations they need to master to succeed in your classroom before you return to the process of providing consequences. Taking the time to do this also supports your relationship with students.

Consequence Documentation

It is extremely important to have a system to record every instance you provide a consequence to a student. As a busy teacher, if you do not record all consequences, you run the risk of forgetting to hold students accountable, thus undercutting your effectiveness.

▸ **Use a clipboard with a tracker:** Many teachers find the easiest system is to carry a clipboard on which they document every consequence they provide. They also use this clipboard to hold sticky notes with their precise directions and document students who go above and beyond during the class period.

▸ **Use a phone application:** Several phone applications track student discipline and incentives. If you find it easy to manipulate, this may be the option for you to track consequences.

No-Nonsense Nurturers do not allow students to erase a consequence. If the class earns an incentive, the whole class gets the incentive. If a student earns a consequence, the teacher understands that he or she must provide the consequence. Otherwise, the teacher is inadvertently teaching students to manipulate the accountability systems in their classroom. Therefore, it's highly recommended to separate incentive and consequence systems. (See page 132 for more on incentives.)

I learned this lesson from one of my third graders when I was a principal in Oakland, California. Timothy had a lot of energy and always got his work done quickly. When he was done with his assignments, he often made it a game to engage other students in his off-task behaviors.

One day, Timothy's teacher sent him to my office, and like always, I engaged him in a conversation. I asked him why he kept ending up in my office when I knew he could do better. On this particular day, Timothy had an interesting answer for me.

"You see, Dr. Klei, I like Ms. Shakes and all, but the trick to her class is just to be good at the end of the day, and then she will remove your consequences. So, you see, if I am good during science (the last forty-five minutes of the day), then she never ends up calling my mother!"

There it was, from the mouth of babes! That day after school, I shared my new learning with Ms. Shakes and she instilled a new policy the next day. Timothy tested the new policy of not being able to earn back his consequences and engaged in off-task behaviors that day. Ms. Shakes was due to call his mother about his behaviors that evening when I saw him in my office. His reflections were a little different from the day before.

"Well, I guess she means it. She really isn't going to give them back to us (referring to consequences he had received). I should act better from now on, Dr. Klei, or my mother will get me! She tells me every morning when I get out of the car that she expects me to behave and make the right choices—and she means it!"

continued →

I didn't see Timothy again for making poor choices in class. Although he almost always got his verbal warning and often missed part of his recess for a stay-in-the-game conversation with Ms. Shakes, he didn't want her to call his mother about his misbehaviors, so he judiciously monitored his choices.

While Ms. Shakes still needed to make sure Timothy had the appropriate work to keep him challenged, he taught both of us a valuable lesson that changed how we thought about consequences. Interestingly, No-Nonsense Nurturers also learn the same lessons about consequences and incentives; they realize early in their careers that consistency and predictability with these systems help build trust, an instrumental part of their life-altering relationships. When teachers have a choice to remove consequences because of subjective behaviors, they remove consistency and predictability from their accountability systems through judgment and negotiation. Without consistency, your accountability systems will fail.

It is important to monitor students you redirect. At the first opportunity, No-Nonsense Nurturers positively narrate students' on-task behavior. This communicates to students that you will recognize them for appropriate as well as inappropriate behaviors.

Supportive Strategies for Students Who Challenge Consequences

It's not uncommon for some students to get upset when you provide a consequence. These outbursts can be very stressful for the teacher and can negatively impact the classroom culture for students. Proactively teaching a "keep it small" mindset will help to eliminate or diminish the number of possible interruptions in your classroom.

Teacher: "If you earn a consequence for your behavior because you have chosen to not follow my directions, I expect you to keep your reaction small. By *small* I mean you are to remain calm and not make any verbal or nonverbal comments. If you feel you were unfairly singled out, feel free to talk with me about it at the next break or after class. If you choose to make a big deal out of getting a consequence, such as arguing, yelling, or refusing to follow the redirection, you will choose to immediately get the next consequence on our accountability hierarchy. My job is to keep us all safe and on track in this classroom. While I might make mistakes from time to time with regard to consequences, I take that job very seriously and care very much for each of you. I promise to do my very best to be fair to everyone. Are there any questions?"

Consider practicing this skill by role-playing scenarios with your class on how to keep it small. By teaching students to keep it small, you are accomplishing several of these important goals.

▶ You are letting students know you are prepared to support anyone who attempts to take away from the positive classroom culture.

▶ You are letting students know you are open to talking with them if they feel unjustly singled out, and you can take appropriate steps to remedy any situation.

▶ You are teaching students they can control their behavior and do not have to allow situations to escalate even when upset. Students can approach you and talk through their feelings or concerns.

Regardless of using this mindset, four behaviors seem to challenge teachers and administrators the most.

Four Common Challenging Behaviors

The following are the most common behaviors educators report finding challenging (Klei Borrero & Canter, 2018).

▶ Students who talk back

▶ Students who argue

▶ Students who continually disrupt

▶ Students who are openly defiant

These behaviors are not unique, and students exhibit them for very good reasons. Many students who talk back, argue, or become defiant do so because they have felt silenced in school or even dehumanized in classrooms throughout their academic careers. While subconscious for some students, others choose these behaviors and may not learn from teachers who do not care about them (Duncan-Andrade, 2007; Kohl, 1994). When working to mitigate and eventually eliminate these behaviors, No-Nonsense Nurturers address the reasons for these behaviors as an essential part of relationship building.

No-Nonsense Nurturers use specific strategies in their responses to each type of challenging behavior. It is important to remember that students you find challenging are the ones you have the most to learn from and need the most from you so they don't continue to fall through cracks in the education system. These students just want and need to be humanized. They want to be noticed, cared for, and loved.

Challenge yourself to find patience when you think you have none and find something you absolutely adore about each student. This will help you focus on students in a more caring way and eventually transform them in your eyes.

> I had a teacher once tell me about a student who was very challenging for her. She even admitted that she didn't like this student very much. After helping her see why it was important to humanize this young girl and supporting her with relationship-building strategies, she came to me a few months later and said, "When I decided to like her, I ended up falling in love with her. She is now one of my most engaged students." With a little venting, some strategic support, and a lot of perseverance, this teacher made school a positive place for a student who may otherwise have fallen through the cracks.

The following are a few strategies to deal with some of the most common and challenging behaviors you might face in your classrooms to support you on your journey as a No-Nonsense Nurturer.

Students Who Talk Back

After receiving a consequence, some students will talk back. The student might say something like "I didn't do anything" or "You are always picking on me." What is the best way to handle this?

Provide a consequence, and then narrate two to three students. Because the student's action is not in his or her best interest and disruptive to the classroom, calmly give the student the next consequence in the accountability hierarchy using your strong teacher voice. "Jenn, I understand you are feeling frustrated, but you have now earned your next consequence. You need to silently get started on your work now. I know you can do this, and if you need help, all you need to do is raise your hand."

Move away from the student and walk around the classroom, immediately narrating two to three students so Jenn has examples of what the direction looks like. If Jenn gets to work in the next three to five minutes, narrate about her.

While you are providing a consequence to a student, don't hover. Allow the student some time to think through his or her options and make a decision. If you hover, the student might have to save face with his or her peers and try to continue to challenge or engage with you.

Students Who Argue

Students who talk back sometimes escalate into students who argue. After you provide a consequence for off-task behavior, Jenn may have learned that by getting agitated and verbally engaging you in an argument, she can manipulate you and keep you from providing the consequences she earned. This is a perfect time to execute a time-tested strategy called the *broken record*.

The broken record strategy is useful to deescalate situations in which students become upset (Canter, 2010; Canter & Canter, 1976). The key to using this strategy is to remain calm and just keep repeating your precise directions for students.

When a student is attempting to argue with you, use your strong, low, calm teacher voice and simply repeat your directions several times, like a record stuck on a turntable. By repeating what you expect, you maintain control of the conversation and your calming voice calms the student down, as in the following example.

> **Jenn:** "You are always picking on me."
>
> **Teacher:** "Jenn, I get that you are frustrated. The directions are to work silently on the assignment. Get started."
>
> **Jenn:** "But you never give me a break."
>
> **Teacher:** "I get it. Jenn, get started on your work. You know how to do this."
>
> **Jenn:** "You don't get me."
>
> **Teacher:** "Jenn, I understand you are frustrated. I care too much about you to let you leave your work. Silently get started on the assignment."
>
> **Jenn:** "But . . ."
>
> **Teacher:** "Jenn, silently get started on your assignment."
>
> **Teacher (moving away and narrating):** "Ronardo is silently working on his assignment. Kirsten is working silently . . ."

Although this works more often than it doesn't, if you don't have success with this scripted scenario, try moving closer to Jenn and, if necessary, give her an additional consequence for disrupting the class. A teacher should use the broken record strategy (instead of just moving to the next consequence) when a student tries to engage after the teacher issues a consequence. If you move too quickly to the next consequence, a student moves through your accountability hierarchy too quickly. When students try to argue, it is their way of trying to do one of two things: (1) be heard because you have consequenced the wrong student or (2) engage, hoping you will take away the consequence.

At the end of class, check in with Jenn with a stay-in-the game conversation or restorative conversation. Ask what is bothering her. Let her know those types of outbursts will not be tolerated in your classroom, and you care too much about her to let her miss out on her education. Make sure she knows she has a voice in your room, but you want her to use it in ways that are constructive to her working space and the working environment of others.

Students Who Continually Disrupt

Some students can cause repeated disruptions. If, after you provide an initial consequence from the classroom accountability hierarchy, they continue to disrupt the learning environment, be sure not to fall into the following common traps.

- **Resignation:** Ignoring the student's behavior
- **Frustration:** Continuing to administer consequence after consequence until you finally remove the student from class

  Instead, help the student redirect his or her behavior by doing the following.

  - Have a brief stay-in-the-game conversation with the student. If the student continues to disrupt more than once over a few minutes, conduct a ten- to thirty-second stay-in-the-game conversation to help the student redirect his or her behavior back on task. In this brief discussion, be sure the student understands the following two key points.
    - *Your concern*—You are concerned about the student and his or her academic achievement.
    - *Your high expectations*—You believe in the student, and you will not tolerate this behavior because it doesn't represent the student's potential. You care too much about the student and his or her success to ignore this obstruction.
  - Handle the stay-in-the-game conversation depending on the student's age.
    - With elementary students, have a quick desk chat. Choose an appropriate moment and go to the student's desk to have a short redirecting

conversation. This proves the least distracting for your class.

▸ With middle and high school students, move them away from the rest of the class. Choose a location away from the student's peers to have your stay-in-the-game conversation. The farther the student is from peers, the less likely he or she will put on a show to save face.

See page 112 for the formula for stay-in-the-game conversations. The following is an example of a stay-in-the-game conversation with a student who is struggling with continual disruptions.

> Michael has disrupted the class two times in the first twenty minutes by trying to engage his peers in inappropriate chatter. After the second consequence, the teacher engages Michael in the following stay-in-the-game conversation.
>
> **Teacher:** "Michael, meet me in the hallway. I will be there as soon as I am finished helping Angela."
>
> Twenty seconds pass, and then the teacher meets Michael in the hallway after positively narrating the rest of the class. The teacher continues to keep her eye on the class while standing in the doorway threshold with Michael.
>
> **Teacher:** "Michael, you have earned two consequences for talking today. You are supposed to be working on your assignment independently. What's going on?"
>
> **Michael:** "I'm bored. I did what you asked me to. Why can't I just talk to my friends?"
>
> **Teacher:** "You're bored? Thanks for letting me know. When we go back in, I will give you feedback so I can continue to challenge you on this assignment, but that isn't an excuse for disrupting your peers. I care too much about you and too much about them to have their education compromised. How are we going to fix this?"
>
> **Michael:** "I get it. I get it. I need to give students their space. But you could make this more interesting."
>
> **Teacher (chuckling):** "I hear you, Michael. I will keep that in mind with tomorrow's lesson as long as I see A+ work from you. Let's get back in there and get back to work."

The teacher and Michael re-enter the classroom. The teacher positively narrates two students as she and Michael make their way to his desk to review his work. The teacher then moves to Michael's desk to review the assignment and give him feedback.

Students Who Are Openly Defiant

Openly defiant students—those who repeatedly refuse to follow your directions and cause repeated disruptions in your classroom—while less common, are typically the most stressful for teachers to deal with. Open defiance is a learned behavior, and the key here is to help students learn a positive replacement behavior in your classroom.

Open defiance usually happens after you have redirected a student and he or she becomes extremely angry. At that point, the student is typically overtly testing your authority. How you respond is critical to earning the respect of that student and your class.

When the student chooses to become openly defiant, the whole class will be watching with a laser focus to see what happens and how you handle it. You must demonstrate to your class that you will not allow this type of behavior. You also need to ensure the defiant student knows you care too much about him or her and about the culture of your classroom to let any anyone misbehave in this manner. The following is the five-step formula for working with a student who demonstrates defiance.

1. **Stay calm:** No matter how upset the student gets, you must stay calm. In fact, the angrier or more upset the student gets, the calmer you need to be. Your calming voice will keep the class calm and help the student settle down as well.

2. **Use a firm, strong tone for redirecting while implementing the broken record strategy:** As previously discussed on pages 125–126, the purpose of using this strategy for students demonstrating defiance is to try to get them focused on their choice while you use a calm voice.

3. **If the student continues to be defiant, remove him or her from the classroom:** Defiance is a serious disruptive behavior and you must address it with a meaningful consequence, namely, sending the student to the designated administrator or counselor at your school, so he or she can calm down. If you allow the student to stay in your classroom, you are sending the message to your class that it is OK to defy your authority and disrupt student learning. The ensuing fallout could seriously jeopardize your classroom culture.

4. **If the student refuses to leave, have a backup plan:** A student you find especially challenging may refuse to leave your classroom. Don't fall into the trap of continuing to direct the student to leave. The resulting "No, and you can't make me" response will make this exchange a fruitless exercise. You know you cannot physically remove a student from your room, nor should you. More important, the student and his or her peers know this as well. If you try to stand toe-to-toe with the disruptive student by demanding he or she leave, you will put yourself in a no-win position. The longer the verbal exchange continues, the more your authority will diminish. No-Nonsense Nurturers know they must have a backup plan to ensure they get the support they need to remove a highly disruptive student from their classroom (Canter, 2014; Charles, 1999).

   The backup plan is usually a system that enables you to contact an administrator or support staff who will safely remove the student. A backup plan is a major confidence builder for teachers. If you do not have such a plan, you will be reluctant to work with highly disruptive students, fearing that if the situation gets out of hand, you will be unable to deal with it. However, what happens if you call the office or security and you cannot reach anyone? What if the alerted support doesn't show up as promised? Simply acknowledge this communication glitch by stating the obvious. Then tell the disruptive student what will happen if he or she still chooses not to exit your classroom, as in the following example.

   > **Teacher:** "Keith, it seems there is not a support person available to remove you from the class right now. This gives you another chance to make the right decision and walk to the principal's office. I care too much about you and our classroom environment to have this level of disrespect. If you choose to stay, I am going to continue the lesson, and as soon as I am able, I will get support to remove you from the class. Consider your actions and choices." (The teacher then begins narrating students who are on task before continuing with the lesson.)

5. **Have a restorative conversation before the student returns to class:** Because a student who demonstrates defiance will need to be removed from your room to calm down, having a restorative conversation is an important relationship builder. Students will likely understand that their actions are unacceptable but your understanding is also important. Giving students a voice during this conversation before you start brainstorming

solutions is essential. Be sure students understand that you do not hold a grudge because of the outburst, and you are excited to have them back in class. During this conversation, identify some of the qualities you admire about these students. Focus on their assets, so they can use those in your classroom instead of defiant behavior.

Remember, when working to alter the behaviors you find most challenging, you must prioritize your relationships with students exhibiting these behaviors, work to understand why they are behaving this way, and help them replace the behaviors with their voice. By taking the time to understand and humanize students you find challenging, you alter everyone's environment and create a more productive space for the whole class.

Consequences for Students With Additional Needs

For students with additional needs, you may need to make adjustments to how you provide consequences. Be sure to read for any necessary accommodations in the student's 504 plan or IEP. If accommodations are not stated, then assume the student can participate in your classwide accountability system, but begin collecting data if the student has reactions, such as the four we just reviewed, that make you question if he or she needs additional support.

A few simple adaptions for students who are particularly sensitive to consequences include the following.

▶ Give the student consequences privately.

▶ Place a sticky note on the student's desk at the beginning of every period, and track consequences and incentives on the sticky note.

▶ Individualize your accountability system with timed check-ins (that is, every ten minutes verbally or nonverbally note to the student how his or her behavior is positively or negatively affecting the academic experience).

▶ Teach a special minilesson on ways to react to consequences. Many students have never been taught the appropriate reaction to a consequence. Teaching a lesson on reactions and then reinforcing these reactions can be a powerful skill for school and life.

While teachers commonly use these modifications in behavior plans and functional behavior assessments, No-Nonsense Nurturers use these accommodations as a regular part of their practice when necessary to support students.

It is important to note that many 504 plans and IEPs do not have notations about behavioral modifications. So, there is likely no need to change anything about the four-step model, including the process of providing consequences.

Guidelines for Giving Consequences in a High-Functioning Classroom

Most teachers find that if they consistently give consequences and build life-altering relationships with students, the need to give consequences diminishes significantly as the year progresses. At this stage, using less direct, subtler responses can quickly redirect wavering students to get back on task. However, these strategies are only effective when you have a high-functioning classroom, that is, 90 percent of students consistently engaged and on task (Klei Borrero & Canter, 2018).

For example, rather than verbally redirecting students or providing consequences, you can use one of the following simple strategies (once you have already established a no-nonsense nurturing classroom with high expectations).

- **Give "the nod":** If a student is off task or mildly disruptive while you are teaching, nod while making eye contact with the student. This will get the student's attention and clarify that you expect him or her to get back on task.

- **Mention the student's name:** During the lesson, mention an off-task student's name, such as: "I want everyone, including Leah and Heidi, to think about what the author's message was in the last paragraph."

- **Use proximity:** When a student is off task, step into close proximity to him or her as you continue teaching or monitoring the class. If needed, place a hand on the student's desk to draw his or her attention to the lesson.

Providing consequences can be difficult for many teachers, but remember, this is a mindset. If you think consequences are difficult, you are likely thinking of them and using them as punishment instead of as relationship builders. If you approach consequences with your students' best interests in mind, consequences become easier because you are supporting students to be self-disciplined young adults.

Consequences help you (and your students) establish boundaries and build trust and consistency for a safe and nurturing classroom culture.

While consequences are a time to build relationships with students by teaching them self-discipline, good decision making, and to care about their education, incentives are a fun way to promote collaboration and care among students. The second part of your accountability system is setting up an incentive system.

Incentives

Like consequences, incentives can be tricky for some teachers to implement. Questions about intrinsic verses extrinsic rewards come into play. What to incentivize students for or what should just be expected are challenging philosophical questions teachers must answer and grapple with. In the end, the No-Nonsense Nurturers we studied used incentives to build collaborative, supportive environments for all students. Teachers did not individualize incentives in these highly effective classrooms, rather students earned them as a class to encourage support, communication, and collaboration among peers (Klei Borrero & Canter, 2018). This part of the accountability system is not only about teachers building relationships with students but also a bridge for students building trust and relationships with one another through their collaborative efforts.

The following sections discuss the benefits of a classwide incentive system, how to set up a system of incentives in your classroom, and how to address incentives for students with additional needs.

Benefits of a Classwide Incentive System

A classwide incentive system can come in many shapes and sizes, but when executed well, it has several benefits for your classroom culture, such as the following.

▸ **Adds impact to verbal recognition:** When you monitor student behavior and observe students following your directions, verbally recognize their behavior through positive narration and, when appropriate, a point toward the class incentive (Klei Borrero & Canter, 2018). For example: "Esteban has silently finished his first page and is moving on to his second. We have had 100 percent engagement for several minutes. That is a class point."

▸ **Utilizes positive peer pressure:** You may find that middle and high school students do not want to be called out for being on track for fear that their peers may frown on their individual compliance. A classwide incentive system enables you to counter some of the negative peer pressure. When you enable on-task students to earn points that help their classmates achieve an incentive they want, you defuse the likelihood that their peers will look down on them. In fact, just the opposite typically happens. Students will encourage their peers to keep up their on-task behavior, exerting positive peer pressure.

▸ **Helps ensure consistency:** Providing positive recognition is critical to creating a classroom culture where students are motivated to learn. An incentive system supports teachers by consistently providing positive feedback to students. In addition, if you use a classwide points system, you can review a record of how many times you provide positive feedback to students by simply looking at the total points the class earns. If the total is too low, that is a cue to increase your positive recognition. Too high? Adjust accordingly.

▸ **Develops perseverance and stamina:** Understanding how to persevere and earn incentives (a promotion at work, a better job, successful relationships with family and friends) is also an important skill for students. Setting up incentive systems in which students have to work together over a period of time helps develop a sense of perseverance, stamina, and collaboration to work for a set period of time to earn something important or desired.

▸ **Builds community and sense of collective efficacy:** Classwide incentives build community and collective efficacy among students. This is particularly powerful in classes with students from traditionally disenfranchised communities. The idea that they can work and succeed together—to achieve something amazing—builds a sense that they can accomplish great things together as a team.

Incentive System Setup

Setting up an incentive system can be a powerful culture builder in your classroom; however, it takes a bit of planning to set it up correctly. Keep each of the following six tasks in mind as you set up a system that serves you and your students in building a collaborative culture.

1. Identify the behavior or academic target.

2. Market the incentive system.

3. Set a reasonable time frame.

4. Select the incentive.

5. Track student progress.

6. Celebrate meeting the goal.

Identify the Behavior or Academic Target

To start your planning, identify a behavior or academic target or two that you want your class to work on together. At the beginning of the year, your target might focus on exhibiting100 percent on-task behavior, entering the classroom quickly to begin the Do Now, or establishing quick transition times. As the year progresses, your targets might focus on 100 percent of students in their seats before the bell rings, 100 percent attendance, or 100 percent homework turned in. As students meets these goals, make your targets more academic so students are encouraged to support one another's learning. Your targets might also focus on whole-class mastery of a certain standard, everyone raising his or her benchmark scores by at least 10 percent, or everyone taking the American College Test (ACT) or Scholastic Assessment Test (SAT).

Market the Incentive System

Market the concept of an incentive system to students. Include an introduction and rationale as to why you think the system is important, and then give points as part of your positive narration routine or when students meet your expectations. Track behavior and academic goals accurately and consistently, and most important, root for your class to earn the incentive as a way of building and sustaining positive momentum and relationships.

However, if you teach multiple classes in a day, be aware of competitions among classes to earn the incentive. While initially this serves as a strong motivator, different classroom chemistries might cause some classes to earn the reward faster than others. If this is the case, students may quickly figure out they will never earn the incentive, and the power of the incentive system is lost. Instead, always set a number of points that each class or period needs to earn so all classes can earn the incentive.

Set a Reasonable Time Frame

Time frames for earning an incentive are important because your follow through supports your relationships with students. Many students are used to teachers who make promises and then never follow through or take too long to follow through. Don't fall into that trap. Always stick to your word and follow through with both incentives and consequences to build trusting relationships with students.

Table 5.2 offers time frames for earning incentives based on students' ages, along with the number of points students should aim to earn during each hour or class period.

Table 5.2: Suggested Time Frames for Earning Incentives

Grade Level	Time Frame to Earn Incentive	Goal for Points (per Hour or Class Period)	Points to Be Earned for Incentive
Kindergarten through second grade	One to two days	Five to ten per hour	Fifty to seventy-five
Third grade through fifth grade	Three to five days	Three to five per hour	Fifty
Middle school	Weekly	Three to five per period	Twenty-five to thirty
High school	Every one to two weeks	Three to five per period	Forty to fifty

*Visit **go.SolutionTree.com/behavior** for a free reproducible version of this table.*

Following are suggestions for when to give class points. While not an exhaustive list, you might want to consider these situations for positively narrating students and giving class points.

- ▸ Students' voice levels meet your expectation for an extended period.

- ▸ All students are on task while you are conducting instruction.

- ▸ Students work cooperatively in groups.

- ▸ Most students volunteer to answer questions.

- ▸ Students answer difficult or rigorous questions.

- ▸ Students take academic risks.

- ▸ Students enter the classroom silently.

- ▸ A new transition goes smoothly and quickly.

- ▸ Students walk silently through the hallway.

- ▸ Assessment scores significantly improve.

- ▸ Students have perfect attendance.

- ▸ One hundred percent of students turn in their homework.

To note, utilizing positive narration in conjunction with a classwide incentive system can dramatically increase your influence on student success, especially at the beginning of the school year or when re-norming your classroom. As you positively narrate students, the percentage of them following directions will increase significantly. As positive behaviors increase, students can earn class points toward a meaningful incentive.

Select the Incentive

As the teacher, you need to identify the target and time frame before you invest students in the incentive they choose. It is critical that students invest in the incentive. What is the best way to do this? Ask them! Be sure, however, to set parameters. Incentives should be low cost or no cost and not take a lot of time away from instruction. Be sure the incentives are interesting to everyone in the class. Choosing an incentive can be as easy as listing ideas on the board and then voting, or having incentive choices as an extra question on an exit ticket.

Table 5.3 shows some possible incentive ideas.

Table 5.3: Possible Incentives

Grades K–5	Grades 6–12
Extra center time or collaborative group time	Student choice of a free pass. • Homework pass • Bathroom pass • Locker pass
Extra physical education time	Listening to instrumental music during their Do Now or exit ticket work
Lunch or a nutritional snack with the teacher	Listening to their favorite music during independent work time
Choice time or extra time with mathematics or literacy games	Five minutes of free time at the end of class
Additional time during the day for teacher to read to the class	A nutritional snack

Five extra points on the next quiz	Lowest quiz grade dropped Five extra points on next quiz Notes for a test or quiz
Short movie related to the subject area	Short movie related to the subject area
Extra day or weekend to complete a project	Extra day or weekend to complete a project
Positive phone call home	Positive phone call to family member of student's choice
Technology time: Extra time set aside to play favorite academic games or work on technology-based projects	Technology time: Extra time set aside to play favorite academic games or work on technology-based projects

*Visit **go.SolutionTree.com/behavior** for a free reproducible version of this table.*

Find incentives that work for you and your students. While educators debate at length *intrinsic* versus *extrinsic* motivations and incentives, working toward these mini challenges or goals can infuse enthusiasm that builds community and translates into motivation and joy throughout your classroom.

Track Student Progress

Once you establish the incentive and time frame, you need to keep track of the points students earn. You might want to keep the points earned in a public place so students can also track their progress. Each time students meet one of their targets, they earn a class point. (Other trackers include dropping a marble in a jar, keeping a tally on the whiteboard, moving a clothespin up a meter stick, and so on).

Note that if students earn a point, you cannot take it away. If a student is off task or disruptive and narration does not work, then provide a consequence to that student. Once students earn a point, an incentive, or a consequence, it should remain. This provides consistency in your classroom, which supports a sense of social justice and fairness.

Celebrate Meeting the Goal

When students meet their goal, be sure to award the incentive and celebrate with students as quickly as possible. Some teachers, depending on the incentive, have celebrations ready for whenever students earn them, while others set up a specific time of day. I suggest, however, that teachers avoid Friday afternoons. While it seems like a good time, this is also a time when your class is likely to be more distractible because of the impending weekend. Teachers often end up feeling torn, for if students are receiving more consequences on Friday afternoons, it is harder for them to then celebrate achieving an incentive. Just as No-Nonsense Nurturers don't erase consequences, they don't take away students' earned incentives. However, giving the incentive during a time when there might be multiple off-task behaviors can feel awkward, so plan for a different time other than Friday afternoons. Some teachers like to use Monday mornings for the incentive because it also acts as a motivator for getting everyone to class on time.

> A teacher in Charlotte, North Carolina, used one of my favorite class incentives. Kristen Schnibbe asked her sixth-grade students what they would like to earn as an incentive. One of her students jokingly said, "We want to see you do cartwheels in the cafeteria at lunchtime." The class giggled, but Ms. Schnibbe surprised them when she replied, "I can do that!"
>
> Her students were amazed and very excited about the possibility. After the class earned twenty-five points by turning in 100 percent for homework and 100 percent for on-task behaviors, during the lunch period, Ms. Schnibbe did cartwheels on the stage in the cafeteria. This took less than a minute. The students, however, were beyond excited. It was so successful, in fact, that several other teachers asked if they could allow their students to be part of the incentive as well! This simple, free incentive proved to be much more valuable than the traditional pizza party we so often sway teachers from using because of the expense. Be creative! Have fun with it and make it a relationship builder! (K. Schnibbe, personal communication, November 16, 2011)

When students have mastered the classroom policies, procedures, and routines, and off-task behavior is of little concern, quickly redesign your incentive system to focus on academic goals the class can achieve and celebrate together.

Incentives for Students With Additional Needs

Incentives for students with additional needs can vary widely. While No-Nonsense Nurturers typically use incentives for classwide successes, you may have students who will benefit from individual accommodations. A likely accommodation may be (but is not limited to) a student needing an individualized incentive system to support his or her behavioral or academic goals.

These systems for individual incentives might look like frequent check-ins with the teacher; a sticker chart in the corner of an elementary student's desk to note each good decision he or she made; or daily or weekly check-ins with a guidance counselor for middle or high school students to ensure they are achieving smaller goals, passing classes, and meeting credit requirements for graduation. Depending on the student, discuss the appropriate incentive plan with the special education teacher and always consult the student's IEP or 504 plan for ideas and noted requirements.

Conclusion

In this chapter, you explored how accountability systems are relationship builders that can incorporate structures that feel safe, predictable, and socially just for students. By following the guidelines, consequences and incentives can support your relationships by building trust and collaboration. In addition, consequences and incentives support your efforts to set high expectations in a safe learning environment for everyone. The next chapter offers additional strategies to build life-altering relationships with students and their families—the cornerstone of your journey to becoming a No-Nonsense Nurturer.

Video

This brief video montage was designed for readers to view the steps of the No-Nonsense Nurturer four-step model individually and in teams. Scan this code to view No-Nonsense Nurturers as they demonstrate accountability systems in action.

Accountability Systems in Action

www.ct3education.com/book/accountability-systems

Reflection Activities

The reflection activities on pages 140–141 are designed to help you reflect on your current professional practice and support your journey to becoming a No-Nonsense Nurturer. You may choose to complete them individually or in teams.

Planning Accountability Systems

Take ten to fifteen minutes to consider the following questions. If needed, use the questions to support your planning for modifying or creating accountability systems in your classroom.

What are the essential elements for implementing an effective consequence system? Incentive system?

Do the students in your classroom care about consequences? Are you giving too many warnings or reminders? Do students take consequences seriously? Are you using consequences as opportunities to build relationships with students?

If they exist, how are incentives working? Are they collaborative? How can you use incentives to support your relationships with students and among your students?

Do you need to modify the accountability system in your classroom? Why?

How do precise directions, positive narration, and accountability systems contribute to overall relationship building with your students?

Role Play

Ask a teacher you respect to role-play a student you both know and find particularly challenging. With your colleague role-playing that student, give him or her precise directions, positive narration, and then consequences. Have your colleague really test you and give you feedback on how you can better provide consequences and build a relationship with the student. By practicing, you will feel far more confident when a student you find challenging tests your authority.

In a separate scenario, role-play a stay-in-the-game conversation or a restorative conversation with your colleague portraying a student you find challenging. Get feedback from your colleague as to how you can better relate to the student or find empathy in what he or she is struggling with in your classroom.

Write a response to your role-playing experiences in the following space.

CHAPTER 6

Build Life-Altering Relationships

This book emphasizes the importance of building relationships to support your classroom management, culture, and overall success as an educator. The first three steps of the No-Nonsense Nurturer four-step model—(1) give precise directions, (2) use positive narration, and (3) implement accountability systems—do two things. First, they lay the groundwork for building relationships with students. The model gives students the permission to expect structure, routine, and clear expectations in the classroom, which in turn builds trust and sets the stage for building strong relationships. Second, these steps buy you the time needed to build the deep relationships with students necessary for them to engage in meaningful learning in your classroom.

By implementing the first three steps, teachers and students are learning in a structured, calm, positive, and caring environment. When implemented effectively and consistently, this model sends the message to students that you are a caring adult who supports and respects them as young people; you are someone they can count on. The first three steps help you establish trust and earn respect so, over time, when students feel more comfortable, they begin to open up, take risks, and authentically engage in learning. This is the path to building life-altering relationships with students, the focus of this chapter. See figure 6.1 (page 144).

All four steps of the No-Nonsense Nurturer model are important and work together toward building life-altering relationships with students. If you only concentrate on giving precise directions, using positive narration, and implementing accountability systems without taking time to build strong relationships with students and their families, your classroom culture will likely fall short of providing a supportive environment for all students. However, if you only rely on building relationships without implementing the first three steps, you will likely lack structure and clarity necessary for rigor and high expectations.

Figure 6.1: Build life-altering relationships.

In this chapter, you will explore what it means to build life-altering relationships and the benefits of those relationships to student growth and learning. This chapter presents strategies you can use with students before, during, and after the school day as well as relationship-building strategies to support students' families. Finally, you will find information on the mindset needed to build effective relationships as well as time management strategies to ensure these activities fit into every teacher's busy schedule.

Benefits of Building Life-Altering Relationships

Relationships are going to form in your classroom. We spend so much time with our students over the course of a school year that it's inevitable. Having productive, healthy relationships creates an environment where everyone wants to engage as a learner, as a teacher, and as a facilitator creating a pathway for learning to happen. Healthy relationships make the classroom a place where students want to come every day not just for learning but because people care about them and want them to succeed. As a teacher, relationships make our work a worthwhile use of our time, and they allow for job satisfaction unequaled in almost any other profession.

Relationships are the cornerstone of a No-Nonsense Nurturer's classroom. Knowing each student as an individual, not just as a young academic, provides valuable information to a teacher who is trying to engage every student, every day. Continuing to learn and understand what is important to students, what motivates them, what challenges them, and what excites or concerns them are all ways to make content and curriculum more relevant and interesting for students. Relationships make the classroom a place of joy, challenge, excitement, and engagement.

Let's continue to examine how No-Nonsense Nurturers build and use their relationships with students and families to support a more productive learning environment. Some of you might already be implementing many of these strategies to support your relationships with students, while others might find the strategies to be worthy additions to their repertoires.

Relationship Building During the School Day

Time is a precious commodity for all of us, especially busy teachers. This section offers some relationship-building strategies you can use during the school day. You may find that you already use some of these strategies, while others may be new. Review each strategy and decide how you might incorporate it into your day.

Distribute a Questionnaire or Survey

An entry point to developing relationships is to distribute a simple survey. On this survey, include open-ended questions for students to answer and give feedback to you on what they like and dislike about school and former teachers; what goals they have for the year; the adult at home who is most important to them; what they like doing in their free time; and so on. The key here is not to just give the questionnaire but also review it carefully and then use what you learn to make authentic connections with students.

For example, after reviewing the surveys, perhaps you notice that your student, Karen, is closest to her grandfather. After her first mathematics test, you tell Karen, "Scoring an 88 percent on our first mathematics quiz is great. Would you mind if I gave your grandfather a call and let him know about your accomplishment?" This lets Karen know two things: (1) You read her questionnaire—something other teachers may not have done in the past—and (2) you care enough about her to reach out to her grandfather to share a bit of notable, positive news. In this situation, it is important to ask Karen if she would like you to reach out before doing so. Getting her approval helps communicate your respect for Karen and is one step toward earning her resect as well. If she does not want you to share with her grandfather, this opens the door for a conversation in which you can learn more about Karen and her family by asking one of two questions: (1) "Is there someone else you prefer I call?" and (2) "Why don't you want me to reach out?"

An additional way to use surveys and questionnaires is for students to survey each other. Teachers often assume students in their classrooms know one another when, in fact, they may not. Have students survey one another for their interests, commonalities, and differences so they can share with each other. Assign students to groups based on needs and interests so they can support one another academically. Building a culture where students feel comfortable with one another can promote an environment in which students are willing to take academic risks and reach higher levels of achievement.

As a teacher and principal, I often used surveys and treasure hunts to identify my students' likes and dislikes. This activity often started with a brief survey of student interests to help me learn a bit more about my students and create collaborative groups. If some students enjoyed science, I might group them together. If students had siblings at the school, they might become a group. I would share their commonalities and then send them to find or build something together with materials around the classroom. For example, I might have students who enjoy science find materials in the lab to build a pulley system together. I might have students who have siblings in school collaboratively map out the best bus routes to get to school, which often engaged them in conversations about restaurants, parks, and places they liked and disliked in their neighborhoods, drawing more connections.

The brief survey and treasure hunt allowed them to compare and contrast experiences, likes and dislikes, and stories, often creating connections and conversations among students who didn't know one another very well. As I listened in, I learned more about students as well. It was a fun, organized activity that I could do on rainy days during recess or when covering a class for a teacher.

Make Sure Students Can Get in Touch With You

No-Nonsense Nurturers embrace their expanded role by allowing students to get in touch with them for support, help, or in case of emergency. For many No-Nonsense Nurturers, this means giving out their cell phone number and regularly checking their school email or voice mail. They tell students to call, email, or text if they need assistance with homework or have a problem and need to talk after school.

A guiding principle for relationship building is that teachers must take the lead. Make positive assumptions about your students and aim for reciprocity with them. For example, at the beginning of the school year, distribute business cards you've ordered from a local or online office supply store. Your card should have your name, title, and the best way for students and their families to get in touch with you—school phone, school email, and possibly your cell number.

When you give students your card, also distribute blank business cards for them to complete and return to you. They can put their contact information on one side and a family member's information on the other. You can extend this activity by having students design their cards featuring the professional roles they hope to hold one day. During lessons, you can make connections to the professions they are working to obtain.

Giving students your business card makes a dramatic statement. It demonstrates that you will be there for them and want to be able to connect with them inside and outside of school.

If you are not comfortable giving out your cell phone number or if district policies prohibit it, be sure to set up alternate communication systems. Some teachers set up a separate Google number (www.google.com/voice) ported to their cell phone (but with a different number) that supports text messaging. The important lesson here, however, is that students and their families must have a clear understanding of how to get in touch with you about questions or concerns. Provide access to students and their families with daily office hours and an email address, and always return messages within twenty-four hours.

Greet Students at the Door

This strategy is simple and sets the tone for the day or class period. Before each class, be sure to position yourself at your classroom door. Greet each student with a smile and a quick, positive comment such as: "Good to see you today," "Looking forward to your contributions in discussion," or "I saw your name in the paper for your cross-country record, congratulations."

Knowing something about each student is important and demonstrates you care about him or her. Doing this before class creates a supportive environment where all students feel welcome and, as a result, more likely to want to learn and participate in your class.

Consider using the 3-H strategy. When greeting students, try using one of the following three Hs.

1. Say *h*ello.

2. Give a *h*andshake.

3. Give a *h*igh-five.

Connect Content to Students

Opportunities for relationship building present themselves while you are working with students in class. Look for these opportunities during whole- and small-group instruction, and make the most of these moments by connecting them back to the learning objective whenever possible. When stories connect to the learning objective and students' lives, students are more likely to remember your lessons. Stories resonate with everyone, especially your students!

Literature and history classes present multiple opportunities for you to connect with and learn more about students. Ask students to connect what they are studying to their own history, culture, and community. Encourage students to use higher-order-thinking skills by making connections while teaching you about their communities and culture. You can promote this through class discussions, writing activities, and connecting current events in the community to what you are teaching. Be open about wanting to learn from your students. Making connections to what is relevant to them not only supports your understanding but also their learning, as in the following examples.

▸ If you know that your students Rico and Eyka are cross-country runners, when teaching distance, time, mathematics, or physics problems, use their names and running times in a problem.

▸ When creating journal prompts or Do Nows, include student names when appropriate.

▸ In science, discuss how using the chemistry students are studying might help solve or connect to a local problem.

Consider and Plan for Students' Personal Needs

One way to communicate you care is to be thoughtful about students' personal needs while in your classroom. While it takes a little bit of time, set up easy routines for students to communicate their needs so you can respond in a timely manner. Consider some of the following ideas.

Hand Signals

Establish communication procedures so students can let you know they need something while not distracting the rest of the class. The method that least interrupts the flow of instruction is for students to use simple hand signals to indicate what they need. The signal should be clearly visible to you yet not distracting for other students, and you should be able to easily respond to the signal with a nonverbal *yes* or *no* nod.

Following are hand signals to support students' personal needs.

▶ Hand raised with one finger = I need to go to the bathroom.

▶ Hand raised with two fingers = I need a sharp pencil.

▶ Hand raised with three fingers = I need a tissue.

▶ Hand raised with four fingers = I need to pick up something.

▶ Hand raised with five fingers = I want to answer or ask a question.

Be sure to include an artifact in your room for students to reference until they learn the hand signals.

Restroom Breaks

Establish times and procedures for students to take breaks. Communicate times when students are and are not allowed to use the restroom, and why you are setting these rules. If students have special needs for restroom use, No-Nonsense Nurturers always accommodate those needs.

Materials

Materials in your classroom are important for students to be successful. Some students are forgetful or struggle with organization, while others face financial difficulties and cannot afford the needed materials. Whether students require a graphic calculator or a pencil, No-Nonsense Nurturers understand the need to make accommodations (and provide learning opportunities) for students so they have the materials they need to be successful.

Share Breakfast or Lunch

Consider inviting a small group of students to eat breakfast or lunch with you in your classroom. In many cultures, sharing a meal is personal and a time to talk and share about your day. At first, students may be reluctant, but as you share about how your day is going or things you look forward to doing over the weekend (thus humanizing yourself), they will join in. Topics for these nonacademic conversations might include sharing interests to find commonalities and noting hopes, dreams, and fears. Topics should deepen your relationship with students in appropriate and joyful ways.

If you bake or enjoy cooking, you might consider sharing your favorite dishes with students over the meal. Cooking for someone shows you care.

Do "Weather" Checks

During the school day, find opportunities to check in with your students about their *emotional weather*. All it takes is a simple question such as, "How are you doing today?" "How is your schoolwork coming?" or "How's it going with your friends?"

This ten- to twenty-second connection shows students that you care and potentially gives you a heads-up about issues to resolve so they don't escalate. If a student lets you know his or her "weather" is not good, find time to talk about it together.

Apologize When You Make a Mistake

Don't hesitate to apologize to students if you make a mistake or have been unfair. As noted in previous chapters, failure is an opportunity to learn. Apologizing identifies a mistake and humanizes you for students. The vulnerability and trust you demonstrate with an apology can be an amazing relationship builder with students. In short, if you make a mistake, admit it and apologize. This not only builds trust but also provides a gateway for students to feel more comfortable with their own mistakes.

Trey was one of the most popular, smartest students I had while teaching sixth grade at Sharonville Elementary. I also happened to know Trey's mother well, as she and I had bonded over one of Trey's older siblings I had taught a few years earlier.

One day, a student with special needs came to me to tell me that Trey had tried to hurt him physically. As the student with special needs told me through his tears, it appeared Trey had also harmed him emotionally. I followed up immediately with Trey to hear the story from his perspective. While admitting that he didn't care much for this student, Trey denied having placed his hands on him. After talking to Trey's mom, she and I believed the other student and Trey should receive consequences at school and at home.

A few days later, Trey was talking to some other students about the incident and how he hated being accused of lying. Several of them approached me to support Trey and expressed that they "wanted the truth to be told." After speaking with these students, it became clear—because of certain time lines—that Trey had been telling the truth and the other student was lying to seek attention.

I felt terrible and immediately apologized to Trey, but I could tell his feelings were deeply hurt. I eventually gathered he was saddened because he not only lost faith in me but also in some of his peers who hadn't believed him. I realized I needed to model my apology for the class, so those students could also repair their relationships.

With Trey's permission, I apologized to him in class the next day. Humbling myself and making everyone aware that I was clearly capable of making mistakes, I hoped to send the message that we all make mistakes but how we handle them is what really matters and is the true test of our character. We had a quieter class that day, and several students followed my lead and apologized to Trey as well, including the student who had made the false accusation. My bond deepened with Trey that day and with other students because of that apology.

To this day, I am still connected with Trey on Facebook—following his journey through college and into the workplace. Every so often when he visits the Bay Area, we make time to have lunch. He is still a young man who challenges how I think about the world, race, and privilege. This is a relationship I believe I benefit from far more than he does.

Relationship Building Before and After School

No-Nonsense Nurturers use every minute they can squeeze out of the school day to build relationships with students; however, they also realize they need to spend time before and after school to connect with students, especially those they find most challenging. Following are some suggestions for how you can check in and connect with students quickly or more at length about various issues.

Quick Touchpoints and Check-Ins

The majority of your before- and after-school interactions with students will be quick contacts, lasting no more than two to five minutes. Following are a few strategies to consider.

Phone Call or Meeting With Students After a Difficult Day (Restorative Conversations)

After you have had a challenging day with a student (for example, having to send him or her out of class or having conflicts over academic performance), call or meet with him or her to work on restoring your relationship (Canter, 2010; Klei Borrero & Canter, 2018). This follow-up can go a long way toward demonstrating to the student that you care and want to start the next day of teaching and learning on the right note—no grudges, just high expectations for the new day.

Positive Boost

When students, especially those you find challenging, have a good day, let them know how pleased you are and how their contributions impacted the classroom with quick face-to-face comments or phone calls. Taking the extra time to shine a positive light on students can shift their paradigm from seeking negative attention to seeking more positive attention.

Phone Call to Absent Students

Show students you care about their well-being with quick calls to their homes after they have been absent for a day or two. Let them know they are missed and, if appropriate, inform them of any assignments they need to make up.

Text Messages

Often text messages are the quickest way to connect with students. You can text them positive messages, check on how they're feeling if they have been sick, or remind them of an assignment due the next day.

Facebook (Social Media)

Some teachers have set up classroom Facebook pages specifically for interactions with students and their families. On the Facebook page, you can check in with students regarding homework, post assignments, and keep in contact with those who move away. Students can post questions, and you or other students in your class can answer them. You can also keep families up to date on homework assignments, study units, and recent class pictures.

Wake-Up Calls

Some students may have the problem of being tardy to class. If so, put the students' phone numbers in your cell phone and give them wake-up calls on your way to work. For upper elementary, middle, and high school students, consider purchasing an inexpensive alarm clock for them. This simple gift demonstrates that you want these students in your class and you expect them to be there on time.

Longer Touchpoints

Some students may need more of your time for myriad reasons. Investing time in your students always pays off and highlights your commitment to them. The following are additional strategies to consider.

Open Classroom Before or After School

No-Nonsense Nurturers let students know they are welcome to hang out in your classroom to complete homework or get extra help or tutoring on assignments. Many students just need a quiet place to work to complete projects and homework assignments. Sharing a space with them while you are both working can develop a sense of caring and achievement. And if a student gets stuck, you are right there to help problem solve.

> Working together with a middle school science teacher in New Orleans, we came up with a plan for her to open her classroom before school every day. During this time, she helped students with questions they had about homework, but she also asked them to support her with tasks such as putting away lab equipment or setting up science experiments for the day. This gave her several extra sets of hands to get organized and time to chat with students and deepen her relationships.

Extracurricular Activities

Attending after-school and extracurricular activities can demonstrate to students that you care about them beyond their academic success. Attending a play, a soccer game, or a church concert communicates to students and their families that you really care about them. These moments, although you may not realize it, can send very memorable and powerful messages to students.

> One of our associates at CT3 mentioned how a teacher attending an after-school basketball game made a huge impression on her daughter, Grace. After mentioning how much she loved basketball, Grace's third-grade teacher came and watched her in a game. Grace is now in the sixth grade and still talks about her favorite teacher attending her basketball game. This made quite an impression on Grace, as this is the only teacher who has come to see her outside the school day. And years later, she is still talking about it! (C. Lupoli, personal communication, June 18, 2017)

As a bonus worth noting, if multiple students play on the same teams or are involved in similar community activities, this may be an opportunity to make connections with more than one student and family at a time.

Something else to consider—you may want to attend students' practices when they aren't at a game. This could be less time-consuming for you to make a connection with students, and you can provide opportunities to check in with them after practice is over.

> While I was coaching a veteran high school teacher in Ohio, the teacher discovered that several of his mathematics students played on the soccer team. As a way to build relationships, this teacher parked his car next to the practice fields. Regularly, he would spend ten extra minutes watching their practice and cheering them on. He reported it worked so well that he could see immediate improvement in behavior and engagement during class. In fact, he planned on using the same strategy with his band students in the following months. He decided to park his car outside the music wing so he could drop by band or orchestra practice on his way home each day. With just a few extra minutes and a little extra planning, these quick touchpoints, centered around student interest, gave him more to connect with his students in class.

Problem-Solving Conferences

If a student presents concerns—behavioral or academic—that are hindering potential success, schedule a meeting and come up with a plan to help get him or her on track. When conducting the conference, follow these seven steps.

1. **Engage with an empathetic mindset:** Come from a place of empathy and caring if a student is struggling in your class. The goal of this conference is not to discipline or punish the student; thus, you want to speak with empathy and caring.

2. **Ask the student for insight into why he or she is struggling:** Don't assume you know why the student is demonstrating inappropriate behaviors or struggling in your classroom. Do some gentle questioning to see if he or she can provide answers.

3. **Decide on steps to support the student:** Determine what you can do to help the student resolve his or her challenges and write it as a plan that you commit to follow.

4. **Focus goals on improved behavior or academic performance:** Focus on how you and the student can improve behavior or academic performance. Examine how your practices influence the student's ability to behave and

react differently going forward. It is common for students to have little to say; some will have a hard time talking about what is going on with them. If this is the case, help the student by pointing out what you are doing to help mediate his or her behaviors and support him or her in making more appropriate choices. Schedule a time to continue the conversations for additional follow-up.

5. **Agree on a plan of action:** Create and agree to a plan that includes steps for both of you to take to improve the situation. Make sure the student knows how the plan will benefit him or her in the future.

6. **Restate your expectations:** No matter what, let the student know that you care too much to let him or her continue to make poor choices in your classroom.

7. **End on a positive note:** Summarize the conference and always end with a note of confidence in the student. Be sure to have a plan on how and when you will check in with the student on his or her progress.

Building life-altering relationships with students takes considerable time, but it will impact student learning and engagement in ways you can only imagine. When teachers demonstrate caring that goes beyond the classroom, relationships built on trust and respect develop, and that supports every learner and teacher in the classroom.

Relationship Building With Students' Families

Creating a partnership with students' families is a key relationship all No-Nonsense Nurturers pursue. Family members are a child's first teachers and the people who surround your students with love and support. While families are different, the importance of family to all students is undeniable. Therefore, eliciting families' help to support your students is key to their success in reaching their goals, both academic and beyond.

I suggest shying away from using the term *parents* when writing or speaking about students. Why? Students come from all different types of families, and many don't live with their parents, but with other caregivers—siblings, grandparents, aunts and uncles, foster families, and multigenerational environments. As No-Nonsense Nurturers, we want to be aware of this and never inadvertently leave out students or make them feel bad about their living situations. By referring to *parents*, we can leave out a student who has lost his or her parents or who lives in a different situation. By referring to *families* rather than parents, we are being inclusive of any caregiver raising the students you serve every day.

Knowing relationships are the cornerstone of No-Nonsense Nurturers' success, let's examine the mindsets many of us hold about families and how we can shift our mindsets to be as empowered and as asset-based as possible. A critical problem educators report facing in their communities is a lack of support from family members (Gibbs, 2005; Langdon, 1996). However, No-Nonsense Nurturers rarely report problems connecting with families. What is the difference? The mindsets No-Nonsense Nurturers hold for the families they serve and the connections they make with them.

Disempowering Mindsets About Students' Families

Research notes that some educators miss opportunities to build relationships with families because they might feel education is not a priority in the students' households (Compton-Lilly, 2003; Lareau & Horvat, 1999; Rothstein-Fisch & Trumbull, 2008). However, this mindset is likely a cultural disconnect or bias educators may hold about their students' families. Educators should closely examine their mindset by considering the following.

▶ Many family members may be reluctant to involve themselves or interact with educators and school staff because they had personally painful or difficult school experiences or because they had negative interactions with their children's teachers or administrators in the past.

▶ Family members may not understand the education system because they are new immigrants to the country, and coming to events is uncomfortable or even frightening for them because of cultural differences or language.

▶ Many family members endure challenges associated with poverty, divorce, mental health, or caring for an ailing family member and as a result, can't attend conferences or school functions. It isn't necessarily due to a lack of concern but availability and immediate priority.

▶ Some family members are more likely to work several jobs, don't have access to childcare for younger siblings, or lack the needed transportation to get to school events.

▶ When family members come to the school upset, confused, or angry, it could be a result of a pattern of experiences with school officials who they believe often don't have the best interests of their children in mind or pressures and challenges they are facing with their family separate from school.

When assessing the previous points, it is also important to consider that the U.S. education system was built on middle-class cultural values and ideals, which can be incredibly difficult to navigate if the families you serve don't share that culture or those cultural norms (Delpit, 2012; Deschenes, Cuban, & Tyack, 2001).

No-Nonsense Nurturer Mindsets About Students' Families

To overcome any possible disempowering mindsets you might harbor regarding family members, take a cue from No-Nonsense Nurturers by doing the following.

▶ Don't assume all family members will give you their trust and support. You may have to earn it by reaching out and building relationships with them. Work to build partnerships with family members so you can better serve students' educational needs. When sending messages to families, be sure they understand any concern you have is to benefit their children.

▶ Make sure your first contact with family members is positive. When you reach out to family members for support, never do so when you are frustrated; instead, do so with a sense of empathy and tell them you are reaching out because you care for and have high expectations for their children.

▶ *Always* assume family members act out of love for their children. Though you might not agree with their decisions, keep in mind that an individual's values, beliefs, and cultural experiences influence child-rearing, so it is a highly personal activity. Reserve your judgment on how families raise their children, and only offer suggestions when asked or when these decisions directly impact their children's success in your classroom.

▶ Approach all interactions with family members knowing they are the most important individuals in their children's lives, and their support is critical to their children's and your success. Family members want to help you. They love their children and want what is best for them. Make sure you present yourself in an approachable fashion. If you present an intimidating or negative attitude, many families will avoid connecting with you.

▶ If family members come to you angry, upset, or confused, show empathy in the situation. Take the family members to a place where they can vent, but listen to the message. Try to overcome the delivery of the message if it is angry or loud, and let them know you are there to try to understand their concerns. Remember, many families have had difficult interactions with public institutions, but if you build relationships with the families you serve, they will rarely, if ever, approach you in anger or with resentment.

▶ If you find family members not engaging in the school environment, try to accommodate their schedule with phone or video conferences. If transportation is an issue, encourage carpooling or have meetings at local churches or community centers that are more accessible for family members. Is childcare a problem? Work with your local high school or church to set up rooms for childcare. Going the extra mile demonstrates care and respect for family situations and gets families involved in the school experience.

No-Nonsense Nurturers spend more time building relationships, and this time investment pays off. Students and their families feel respected and become more engaged, and when you need support, you have partnerships with families and students to rely on. In general, strong relationships make the environment more conducive to learning for students and more enjoyable and less frustrating for you, so the time spent is always a solid investment!

Strategies for Relationship Building With Families

While building relationships with family members is secondary to building relationships with students, it is still very important, and with the students you find challenging, it can be imperative. The following are some strategies to build relationships and garner support from students' families.

Beginning of the Year

Proactive communication with students' families can be extremely beneficial in building trust and respect among the adults in your students' lives. Like No-Nonsense Nurturers, consider making introductory phone calls and using beginning-of-the-year events at school to support your relationships with families. Following are some strategies you can implement at the beginning of the year to build a foundation for relationships with families.

Introductory Phone Calls

No-Nonsense Nurturers understand the importance of building strong, nurturing relationships with families at the beginning of the school year. If a family member's first point of contact with you is a positive experience, it will set an affirming tone for the year and allow momentum to build.

A simple strategy for building positive relationships with families is to make an introductory phone call at the beginning of the school year or at the semester change. These positive calls demonstrate your willingness to go out of your way to reach out to family members, which increases relationship capital and launches your relationships with families on an encouraging note. For introductory phone calls, follow these five guidelines.

1. **Introduce yourself:** Let family members know who you are and your goals for their child.

2. **Solicit input from family members:** How do they feel you can best assist their child? Are there things you should know to support their child to have a successful school year? Ask family members what you should know about their child and if they have any ideas that would be helpful for you as their child's teacher.

3. **Establish parameters for a partnership:** Right up front, let family members know that you want to build a partnership with them to help their child reach his or her potential. Affirm that they play a big part in their child's success and you are looking forward to working with them throughout the school year.

4. **Create lines of communication:** Affirm that your communication with family members will be ongoing. Let them know you'll stay in contact by phone, email, text, or personal notes to ensure they know how their child is progressing. Be sure to invite them to reach out to you as well.

5. **If possible, speak with the student:** If available, introduce yourself to the student and find out what he or she is looking for from you to have a successful school year or semester.

The overwhelming majority of family members and students have not had a teacher who cares enough to call them before school starts or shortly after the school year begins. A nurturing call will go a long way to jump-starting your relationships with a student's family.

Open House

Many schools sponsor a beginning-of-the-year activity like an open house for families to visit classrooms of elementary students or follow the schedule to meet teachers of their upper-grade students. Don't fall into the trap of reviewing a syllabus or rules of the classroom. While you can hand out documents with the student syllabus, policies, procedures, and large project assignments, focus this time on building relationships with families.

Be sure to include activities that make families feel welcome in your classroom. Share a lab experience with them so they get excited about their child's learning. Collect questions from families ahead of time and answer them for the group. Display student work. Enlist families to use their skills to support their child's classroom experience. While time is limited at these events, try to demonstrate to families that you have already learned something about their children, note ways you will build relationships with their children, and let them know how to reach you if they have questions, concerns, or emergencies.

Putting time in at the beginning of the school year is important for building relationships with families, but relationships take work and are ongoing. During the year, the majority of your contact with families will be quick, but sometimes you may need to set aside time for longer meetings with parents or guardians, which takes more planning.

During the School Year

While the previous strategies are better suited to start before or at the beginning of the school year, other strategies can be useful throughout the school year. If your communication is strong and aims to build trust and respect with students' families, everyone will have a more successful year.

Remember to let students know as you communicate with their families. Whether proactive or positive communication or to communicate about consequences from the accountability hierarchy, it should not be a surprise to students that you are communicating with family members. It is a norm you need to create in your classroom, as many students have been taught that communication with families is punitive or a form of punishment. In the case of No-Nonsense Nurturers, the purpose of communication and relationships with families is to support students so the adults in their lives can work together. Following are strategies you can use during the school year to connect with families.

Quick Touchpoints and Check-Ins

As with students, the overwhelming majority of your contacts with family members should only take a few minutes, but even these brief interactions support relationships. Throughout the school year, keep your communication with families positive and predictable by sharing good news about their children in person or by phone, email, or text. Create a schedule so you can communicate consistently, ensuring a strong relationship and partnership to support their children. The following are a few examples.

▶ **Phone messages:** Using the phone to contact families is one of the best ways to build relationships, as it allows for easy two-way communication that brings a personal touch and a sense of empathy and understanding emails and texts rarely convey. The following is an example of a phone message for families.

> Ms. Parks, this is Kristyn Klei Borrero, Diamond's fifth-grade mathematics teacher. I didn't want to bother you while at work, but I thought it was important to leave you a message. Diamond had a fabulous day today and led the class discussion on parallelograms. Please ask her about her day and successes! I hope you are well, and be sure to reach out if you have any questions.

▶ **Emails:** A simple way to deliver good news is to email family members. The nice thing about emails is you can write them at any time, and family members can read them at their leisure. You can also use these positive messages as a record of a student's success for later conferences or when discussing a student's participation in class.

Here is an elementary example.

> Mr. Reynolds,
>
> I just wanted to let you know that Nataki is a star in class, and today she proved it again. She worked hard all day and had a lot to offer during our class discussion on fossils. I am attaching a picture of her from class while she was working hard with her small group. I look forward to her continued success in our classroom.
>
> Please let Nataki know I sent you this message.
>
> Take care,
>
> Kristyn Klei Borrero

Here is a middle and high school example.

> Ms. Reves,
>
> I hope this email finds you well. I wanted to write to make sure you knew the success Ronardo is experiencing in AP biology. I know the year started off a bit rocky for him, but since we last spoke, Ronardo is engaged in class discussions and has gotten a B and an A, respectively, on his last two quizzes. I am very proud of him and the discipline he has shown in his studies, and I wanted to make sure you were aware of his successes.
>
> If I can be of additional assistance, please reach out. And if you would, please let Ronardo know I emailed you.
>
> In partnership,
>
> Kristyn Klei Borrero

▶ **Text messages:** Many of us are guilty of focusing a bit too much on our smartphones these days, but take advantage of the simplicity and efficiency that text messaging can offer relationship-building opportunities with students' families. A simple text message can put a smile on a family member's face and is a quick way to note a student's success. You can also take a picture of the student working hard in class or showing a test score to send with the text. A picture does speak a thousand words!

Here is an elementary example.

> Look who just raised her test score thirteen points! (Attach a photo of student holding the assessment.)

Here is a secondary example.

> Donald's presentation on the Cold War elicited some very interesting questions and connections to today's political environment. He really held the attention of the class! (Attach a photo of student during presentation.)

▶ **Flybys:** When you see family members at drop-off or pickup, take fifteen seconds to give them positive news (Rothstein-Fisch & Trumbull, 2008). Here are two examples.

> I'm really enjoying having Max in my class; he is kind to all the other students and is very helpful.

> Your granddaughter, Barbara, was a rock star in class today. She read a book that was a full grade level ahead.

▸ **Quick consequence and support phone call:** To discuss any issues interfering with a student's educational success, make a quick call. (This may be the "Call family member" consequence on your accountability hierarchy.) Follow these five guidelines, and plan what you will say on the call and how you will elicit family members' support for your efforts to help their child.

    a. *Ask how family members are doing*—Check in with people you are calling. Ask how their day was or if they will be attending the next planned school event.

    b. *Communicate concern for their children's success*— Communicating your concern for their child makes the conversation a lot more productive and comfortable for all of you. Here is an example.

> Ms. Jones, I am calling because Jessica struggled staying on task today and, as explained in the student planner and at the open house, I wanted to reach out with a phone call so you are aware of the choices Jessica made in class today.

    c. *Be objective, not judgmental*—Avoid making judgmental statements about your students. Statements such as "She was completely disruptive," "She continues to be a problem," or "She doesn't try her best" will likely put family members on the defensive. Simply state, in observable terms, your concerns and the student's off-task behaviors, as in the following example.

> Jessica received her first warning on our accountability hierarchy for talking during our Do Now and during independent work time. We then had a stay-in-the-game conversation during part of her recess for blurting out answers during our mathematics lesson. As the day continued, I moved her seat and spoke to her an additional time about making better choices, but the talkative behaviors continued. This is the reason for my phone call to you this afternoon.

d. *Request input from family members*—It is imperative that you give family members a chance to offer suggestions or information that might help explain their child's behavior. Just as with students, family members need to feel that you hear them. Here is an example.

> While I know we have discussed this behavior in the past, Jessica usually works diligently to control her off-task talking in class. Is there anything new I should know about or consider? Do you have any suggestions for me?

e. *Ask family members to speak with their child*—As the conversation comes to a close, request that family members speak with their child. Tell family members that their child can and will be successful in your classroom (especially with their help). It is important that family members know you are not mad at their child or are going to hold a grudge. Make sure they feel appreciated and know you are looking for the best in their child. Here is an example.

> I really appreciate you taking the time to speak with me, Ms. Jones. Can you be sure to let Jessica know that we spoke? I am certain she will do better in class tomorrow, and I look forward to contacting you soon with celebrations of Jessica's hard work in class.

With a little planning, phone calls can support students getting back on track and staying on track. When the student enters your room the next morning, be sure to note that you spoke with a family member, you have high expectations for him or her today, and you are excited to have him or her back in class for a productive day of learning.

Longer Touchpoints and Contacts

While some contacts can be five minutes or less, other contacts with family members take longer. The following contacts can take fifteen to thirty minutes of your time, but if used effectively, deliver a large impact.

Weekly or Monthly Newsletter

Classroom newsletters are an oldie, but a goodie! Sending home or emailing weekly newsletters to families is a great way to keep them informed about what is going on in the classroom (for example, standards being taught, materials needed, upcoming events, and so on). They also let families see their children's names in print for something positive they contributed to the class, as in the following example.

> During last week's discussion on the French Revolution, Joaquin related the experiences of the French during the late 18th century to that of poverty-stricken neighborhoods in our community. This conversation highlighted the importance of studying history and how oppression continues to happen in our local communities today.

While weekly communications are often appropriate in an elementary classroom, monthly communications are often more appropriate at the secondary level. In these newsletters, be sure to highlight overall student success and gains across the class, but also note upcoming units, standards being reviewed, volunteer experts needed, and upcoming assessments to look for, such as Preliminary Scholastic Aptitude Tests (PSATs), SATs, ACTs, and Advanced Placement (AP) exams. Remember, if your students speak more than one language, be sure to translate the newsletter.

Home Visits

Another marker of highly effective teachers is their willingness to meet with families on their terrain (Farr, 2010). You can use home visits for all students, but they are an especially good strategy for when you are struggling to get support from family members of students you find challenging.

The thought of visiting a student's home may seem intimidating at first, but the impact can be powerful. Taking the time and making the effort to sit down with family members in their home sends powerful messages: "I care enough about your child that I will do whatever it takes to support his or her success," and "I value you and your support so much that I will come to you rather than expect you to come to me."

Home visits can be dramatically positive. Frequently, distrustful family members suddenly become major backers of your efforts with their children. In addition, students are often awestruck when you demonstrate such a commitment to their education. As a result, their behavior, commitment, and investment in your class improves dramatically.

A few guidelines for home visits include the following.

▸ **Get the family's permission:** Never simply drop in on a family member at home. Always schedule the visit, and make sure you are welcome. Check with your administrator to make sure he or she approves of home visits.

▸ **Prepare an agenda:** Come to the home visit with an agenda or a lesson plan. Messages during home visits should be generally positive and after the school year has begun, if possible. Bring samples of student work and assessments. Be sure to have a list of positive things to say about the student. If you need to approach any discipline needs, do so with care.

▸ **Keep your safety a top priority:** You may work in an area where the neighborhoods are not safe for you to go by yourself. Consider having another staff member go with you or meet family members at a public location near their home, such as a restaurant or library.

School-Home Contracts

School-home contracts are agreements between you and family members to systematically work together to help their children. These contracts can be extremely motivating for students to get on track. In such agreements, family members agree to support your efforts by following through at home with positive incentives or consequences, depending on how their children are doing in your class. The following eight parameters are for developing a simple agreement with family members. It is important to note that many No-Nonsense Nurturers, particularly in self-contained elementary classrooms, have school-home contracts with all their students and families, while middle and high school teachers tend to use school-home contracts with students who they find more challenging or who are not working to their full potential.

1. **Determine the student's strengths:** Before brainstorming about ways the family can support your efforts, discuss the student's academic and social strengths. Allow family members to do the same. Use this list of assets to support the student with anything he or she might find challenging.

2. **Identify challenging behaviors (if necessary):** Determine the behaviors you need to work on together to support the student with his or her success. Come up with one or two behaviors that are in the student's best interest to improve. These behaviors might include time on task, completing assignments on time, or improved attendance.

3. **Agree on steps to support the student:** Be sure you are prepared with suggestions and ideas to help the student, such as extra tutoring or an individualized behavior plan. You should include all family members' and the student's ideas. In the end, agree on one or two that will best support the behavior you are trying to improve or remedy.

4. **Write a plan:** Script a plan to support the student's behaviors with incentives and consequences attached to the desirable and undesirable behaviors. Be sure to note highly productive behaviors and continue to incentivize those both at home and in the classroom (for example, grit, perseverance, kindness, willingness to help others, and so on).

5. **Determine consequences family members can provide:** Discuss with family members what consequences they can provide their child at home if he or she disrupts class, does not do his or her work, and so on. Typical consequences include the following.

   ▷ Loss of electronic devices (for example, cell phone, video games, television, or computer), so the student can dedicate more time to his or her schoolwork

   ▷ Discussion with family member regarding expectations for school

   ▷ Loss of privileges, so the student can concentrate on his or her schoolwork

6. **Determine incentives (positive consequences) family members can provide:** Discuss with family members what positive incentives they can provide their child at home if he or she chooses to behave as a high-performing student. Typical incentives include the following.

   ▷ Extra time with a chosen family member

   ▷ Extra time playing video or computer games or watching TV

   ▷ Special snacks

   ▷ A special (small) purchase

7. **Determine a communication plan:** Outline how you will communicate the student's daily performance. Most teachers send home a daily note, but with students they find challenging, they might arrange to call, text, or email family members to report on their child's progress for the day. If the student made positive choices, family members reward him or her

with the incentive. If the student made poor choices, he or she receives the consequence so he or she is able to make up the schoolwork from the day.

8. **Review progress:** Agree on a time to review how the student is doing and celebrate his or her progress, or make changes to the plan to further support his or her success.

Problem-Solving Conferences With Families

Talking with family members can sometimes be stressful for teachers (and family members). This is particularly true if there is an issue with the student that you need to address.

No matter what the issue, it is always a good idea to take a moment to think about and write down what you are going to say using the following nine guidelines. Doing this maximizes the probability that you will have a productive interaction with students' family members.

1. **Communicate concern for their child's success:** Always begin your conference with family members by communicating your concern for their child's success. If you want their support, they need to believe you have their child's best interest at heart; they must know you care about their child's success. It is counterproductive to start an interaction on a negative note, such as: "I want to talk with you because I'm really frustrated with how Jasmine is disrupting my class." Instead, communicate your care and concern for their child: "The reason I asked for this meeting is that Jasmine has so much potential, and I'm concerned that she is not doing as well as she can in my class."

2. **Be objective:** Being objective is imperative to your success in soliciting support and advice from family members. Avoid making judgmental statements about their child. Statements such as: "He has a bad attitude," "She's a problem," or "He's lazy" will put family members on the defensive. Simply state, in observable terms, the concerns you have for their child: "She disrupted the class three times today by talking out," "She has not completed her assignments in the last two days," or "She has had four arguments with her classmates this week."

3. **Note the steps you have already taken:** Let family members know the steps you have taken to support their child. Most families want to know that you have tried on your own to help their child before you contact them. Tell them what steps you have already taken: "I've talked with her

about the issue and tried to support her with her peers," or "We've spent time during lunch to discuss better options and reactions for her."

4. **Ask for input:** Families may be all too familiar with teachers who talk at them without respecting their insights or ideas. Ask family members for any ideas they have regarding why their child is having an issue and what can be done to resolve it. Don't forget, family members know their child better than you do and may provide valuable information if you take the time to ask: "I'd love to hear any ideas you have to support Jasmine. I'd be up for trying your suggestions."

5. **Discuss additional steps you can take to help their child:** Present any additional ideas you have to help their child, such as extra tutoring, checking in with family members daily, or in extreme cases, considering an individualized support plan, such as the following example: "I want to make sure I continue to build a relationship with Jasmine, and I think some of her behaviors might be a result of her struggling a bit in mathematics. Could I keep her for thirty minutes after school on Tuesdays and Thursdays? We can spend some time getting to know one another better, but I can also support her with mathematics problems she finds difficult or is struggling to solve."

6. **Determine family members' support:** Work with family members to come up with ideas for how they can support your efforts with their child. This support may focus on making sure the child does his or her homework or providing consequences at home if the child chooses to be disruptive during instructional time, as in this example: "I appreciate your suggestions. I will send a quick daily text letting you know how Jasmine's day went. If you have questions, you can give me a call back. Otherwise, on good days, Jasmine can participate in her after-school activities. On days she struggles, you will be sure to keep her in to study more. Do I have that correct?"

7. **Emphasize the importance of having family members' support:** Let family members know how important their support for your efforts is to their child's success: "You are the most important person in your child's life, and she must know we are working together to ensure she does her best in school."

8. **Plan a time to follow up:** Be sure to determine the next time you will discuss with family members the progress of your combined efforts to help

their child: "I'll email you on Friday with an overview of the week. But expect a quick, daily text from me. I also have it in my calendar that we will meet one month from today to discuss Jasmine's overall progress."

9. **End on a positive note:** When you contact family members regarding a concern you have for their child, they will likely get worried or nervous. Always express your confidence that, as a team, you can support their child: "I have confidence that if we work together, we can help your daughter make better choices and be a successful student."

Whenever appropriate, include the student in your interactions with family members. The student's voice can be powerful and by contributing, he or she can witness how much everyone at school and home cares about his or her success.

There are an endless number of strategies you can use to build positive relationships with students and families; this section just begins to highlight some actions you can start taking tomorrow or in the near future. While this may seem like a lot of strategies, you don't have to do them all to start building strong relationships. Consider which strategies work for you, which fit best into your schedule (with a bit of planning), and which you feel your students would like the most. If you aren't sure, ask them!

No-Nonsense Nurturers spend more time than other teachers building relationships, but this time investment pays off. Students and their families feel respected and become more engaged. When you need support, you have partnerships with families and students to rely on. In general, strong relationships make the environment more conducive to learning for students and more enjoyable and less frustrating for you.

The next section of this chapter highlights how careful time management can maximize the impact of your relationship building with students and families.

Time Management to Maximize the Impact of Relationship Building

Time management is one of the biggest challenges for teachers. It is important to choose how you spend your time and what you prioritize. Will you put all your time into creating the most engaging lesson plans that may, in fact, fail if students are disruptive in your classroom? Or will you allocate some of your time to engaging with students and their families so they know you care about them and their learning?

Time is a teacher's most valuable resource, so using your time wisely can be key for building strong, life-altering relationships with students and their families.

No-Nonsense Nurturers have several strategies for managing time wisely while building relationships.

Preplanning Steps for Building Relationships

When you write your daily lesson plans, set aside times for building relationships with students and their families. The following three preplanning steps will make your efforts more efficient.

1. **Gather data:** Get the phone numbers and email addresses of as many students and key family members as possible. You can do this by collecting the information from emergency medical cards that students turn in at the beginning of the school year or by handing out index or business cards to older students on the first day of school. Getting the correct contact information from students can be a challenge. No-Nonsense Nurturers often tell students that they can choose who receives the first positive phone call of the year. This motivates students to list the correct phone numbers for family members they have the closest relationships with and who, therefore, have the most influence on the students' success in school.

2. **Program your cell phone:** Entering all these contact data into your cell phone allows easy access to them at any time. While this initial work takes some time, it saves a significant amount of time later when you won't have to search for the information. By programming your phone, you can make a quick contact between classes, on your commute home from work, or during class, when you can send a text or a picture of a student demonstrating success to his or her family members.

3. **Establish goals for the frequency of contacts with students and their families:** If you teach in an elementary or self-contained classroom, make it a goal to contact students and their families at least once per month to communicate how each student is doing and to note the positive. Middle and high school teachers should consider communicating with students' families a least every forty-five to sixty days.

Relationship-Building Schedule

Spending time building relationships is analogous to going to the gym or working out. Unless you schedule it into your day, a myriad of other distractions may prevent you from doing it. Therefore, set aside time each day in your calendar and make sure it happens. Following are some strategies for how you can schedule time during the week and on weekends for connecting with students and their families.

During the Week

The work week can be a busy time for both you and students' families. Set priorities for making contact so these opportunities don't fall by the wayside.

▶ **Spend up to one hour per day:** No-Nonsense Nurturers spend up to one hour per day talking with students and their families, especially at the beginning of the school year or when re-norming their classrooms. This is done via phone, email, or in face-to-face meetings.

   How do you find the time? Many teachers use their commute to and from work to communicate with students and their families, while others use part of their planning time or lunchtime.

▶ **Prioritize the students and family members to contact:** Given that your time is limited, prioritize whom you spend time reaching out to each day. The following are some guidelines for determining whom you'll contact.

   ▷ *Students who had a particularly difficult day*—Contacting a family member might be part of your accountability hierarchy, or you might reach out if a student is having a particularly difficult day. This contact can be a quick call to a student's family member to enlist his or her help in redirecting inappropriate behaviors. During these calls, it is important to communicate why you have strong beliefs in the student's ability to succeed in your class and that, as partners, you believe you can support the student to success.

   As a No-Nonsense Nurturer, commit to making as many of these phone calls per day as needed. If you do, eventually you will not have to make as many, and you can spend your time on more positive contacts.

   ▷ *Students you find most challenging*—Contact these students with a positive message if they have had a good day or if they had a difficult day to quickly remind them of their consequences and reset expectations for the following day. You might also want or need to call a family member.

Each week, commit to connecting with two or three of these students and their families at the elementary level and five or six of these students at the middle or high school level.

▷ *Students who have shown improvement*—Reach out with a positive call to at least five of these students and their families per week. These calls tend to be quick, fun interactions. Communicate specific data on how the student has improved and how those improvements will lead to success in the classroom.

▷ *Students you haven't contacted recently*—Reach out with a positive call or in a one-to-one meeting with at least five of these students and their families per week. These are often the students who never or seldom cause disruptions in your classroom, but they still need to hear from you. This type of quick check-in is better suited to a phone call than an email or a text message because it is positive and an energy booster for everyone.

Over the Weekend

Weekend time is valuable, and it is important for you to take the time you need to rejuvenate and achieve balance. However, when you can, weekends are also an opportunity to schedule a little time for building relationships with students and their families.

Saturdays

Take some time once a month to attend a student's sporting, art, community, or religious or cultural event. By attending an event for one student, you will likely run into other students and family members. This is a perfect time to check in and let all stakeholders know you care about your students as individuals, not just as learners.

Several years ago while working with principals, I received a great idea that I still use today. Mr. Wells was a high school assistant principal in Oakland, California, where he also lived with his family. Every Saturday morning, he put his four children, ages four to twelve years, in the car and went to an athletic event to support his high school students. By attending with his children, he got double

continued →

relationship-building points. When Mr. Wells showed up to an event, other high schoolers would often babysit or play with his children, giving them a feeling of belonging and giving him time to talk with families while watching the game or match. (He also got relationship-building points with his wife, who was writing her dissertation and loved getting several hours every Saturday morning to write!) The routine proved beneficial for everyone, and kept him well connected to the community he served.

Sunday-Night Boost

A Sunday-night boost can help students who are struggling academically or who have behaviors you find challenging. Make proactive phone calls so students' transitions into Monday go smoothly. During these phone calls, consider:

▶ Asking students how their weekend went

▶ Inquiring about what students are concerned or excited for in the coming school week

▶ Checking in with students on upcoming projects that are due

▶ Letting students know you are excited to see them in class tomorrow and look forward to a productive week with them and their peers

You might also consider contacting two to three students who do well in your class. By making these calls on Sunday night, you help students start the school week on the right note, and you will get excited for Monday morning.

Relationship Building to Support Students With Additional Needs

Building life-altering relationships is important for *all* students, but is exponentially more important for students with 504 plans, IEPs, and additional needs. Building life-altering relationship with students with additional needs allows you to anticipate challenges and successes they will face in your classroom. Strong relationships allow these students to feel more comfortable and take risks they might not otherwise take. Students who face unique needs and challenges often learn in distinctive ways and perceive situations differently than some of their peers. The relationships you build with these students make a significant difference in who they are as young scholars in your classroom, academically and behaviorally. In addition, the lessons you learn from these students will be an individualized professional development plan for you. The knowledge you gain about yourself and your classroom practices through interactions with students who need accommodations will help you better serve and teach all your future students.

It is equally crucial for you to build nurturing relationships with the families of students with special needs. Unfortunately, school structures may condition these students' families to hear about what their children are doing wrong or how their needs affect others in the classroom (Eccles & Harold, 1993). These families must see you as an advocate for their children and as a team member dedicated to serving their children's needs. Remember that *all* students deserve an equitable education and because *fair doesn't always mean equal*, some students deserve and need more support than others.

As part of your relationship-building strategy, seek out experts to better understand the laws, expectations, and accommodations for every student in your class. Build a high level of trust with these mentors so they can support your strategies with all students, but especially those who may need additional or different supports.

While it does take additional time, relationship building is the cornerstone of your success as an educator. This is time you should enjoy bonding and getting to know students and their families. By incorporating your own family or interests into relationship-building activities, you can often address your personal commitments while getting to know students in more meaningful ways.

For students, relationships are often a prerequisite to learning (Camangian, 2010). For teachers, these relationships can impact the learning of all their future students. Many No-Nonsense Nurturers note that when they build relationships with students and families, they learn much more about themselves as human beings.

Conclusion

This chapter presented strategies for building strong relationships with students and their families, completing your introduction to the No-Nonsense Nurturer four-step model. Take some time now to concentrate on how you want to influence the relationships that profoundly impact both your and your students' success.

Video

This brief video montage was designed for readers to view the steps of the No-Nonsense Nurturer four-step model individually and in teams. Scan this code to view No-Nonsense Nurturers as they demonstrate building life-altering relationships.

Relationship Building in Action

www.ct3education.com/book/relationship-building

Reflection Activities

The reflection activities on pages 177–184 are designed to help you reflect on your current professional practice and support your journey to becoming a No-Nonsense Nurturer. You may choose to complete them individually or in teams.

Build Relationships With Families

Work from your assets when building stronger relationships with students and their families. In the following chart, reflect on your current practices and consider ideas from this chapter to further develop your relationships with students and their families.

Students and family members with whom I currently have strong relationships	Students and family members with whom I want to strengthen my relationships	Relationship-building strategies I currently use	Relationship-building strategies I want to add to my practice	Who I most impact with these strategies

page 1 of 2

No-Nonsense Nurturers invest heavily in their relationships with students and families. Take some time to begin thinking about how you want to build those relationships. Choose three students or family members you want to begin building relationships with, and then brainstorm strategies for getting to know them better. If you get stuck, focus on students you find challenging. Building relationships with them will likely take longer but will go a long way.

Student or family member	How will I get to know this student or family member better?

Create a Relationship-Building Plan

Planning for relationship building is your key to success. Consider the following questions, and then take a few minutes to jot down the relationship-building strategy, the students you will focus on, and the amount of time you expect to spend on relationship building each day next week.

- How much time can I spend each day intentionally strengthening and building relationships with students and families?
- Where do I need to prioritize my efforts? With students? Certain family members? During the day? Before or after school? On the weekends?

	What will I do?	Which students will I focus on?	How much time do I need?
Monday			
Tuesday			
Wednesday			
Thursday			
Friday			
Saturday			
Sunday			

Build Relationships With Focus Students

Each teacher has a student or two he or she finds challenging. Consider the following questions and begin building stronger relationships with these students.

In what ways can you look to the students you currently find challenging to support your development as an educator?

What plans will you put in place to build stronger relationships with these students? Have you tried strategies to build relationships and given up too easily?

What do you know about these students that you can connect with? What do you admire or appreciate about them? (If you don't know of anything, this is an indication you have not spent enough time getting to know them!)

When these students exhibit a behavior you find challenging, what strategies from this chapter will you try to implement?

Reflect and Journal

Take a few minutes to reflect on and answer the following questions.

Relationships

As a No-Nonsense Nurturer, how do I want students to remember me? What types of relationships are necessary for all my students to thrive?

Where are my relationships strong? Why am I succeeding in these relationships?

How can I improve my relationships with my students? Students' family members?

Is there a pattern in my relationship-building strategies?

Students With Additional Needs

As a No-Nonsense Nurturer, how will I be an advocate for students in my class who have special needs? What role will I take on the 504 plan or IEP team to ensure each student's success in my classroom?

What resources do I need to successfully support students in my classroom with 504 plans or IEPs? Where will I begin to seek additional information? The internet? My principal or the onsite special educator? School counselor? Local university?

Support Students With Additional Needs

How will you adapt the No-Nonsense Nurturer four-step model for students with additional needs? In this activity, consider a student with special needs and the accommodations that might maximize his or her success in the general education classroom. As you answer the following reflection questions, incorporate information you have learned throughout this book.

1. Without using the student's name, identify a student who has a 504 plan or an IEP. Briefly describe the student's academic, behavioral, or physical needs.

Academic	Behavioral	Physical

2. What instructional, behavioral, and physical supports does the student require, according to the 504 plan or IEP?

Academic	Behavioral	Physical

3. Consider each step of the No-Nonsense Nurturer four-step model. If necessary, how might you adapt the steps to fit this student's needs?

	Academic	Behavioral	Physical
Step 1: Give precise directions.			
Step 2: Use positive narration.			
Step 3: Implement accountability systems.			
Step 4: Build life-altering relationships.			

Every Student, Every Day © 2019 Kristyn Klei Borrero • SolutionTree.com
Visit **go.SolutionTree.com/behavior** to download this free reproducible.

Conduct a Final Preassessment

It's time for a progress check-in. If you are reading this book while teaching, return to the preassessment you completed in the introduction ("Track Your Progress Toward Becoming a No-Nonsense Nurturer," page 14). Use a different-color pen and make a new set of marks on each continuum to represent where you see yourself today relative to where you began and the star you set as a goal. Be thoughtful and reflective. Notice that your understanding of the questions may have changed as you've progressed through this book. Reflect on the following questions.

In what area have you seen the most growth in your practice?

Are there any areas where you have already reached your goals? To what do you attribute your success thus far?

Putting It All Together

Hopefully this book has inspired you to continue to work on your practice as an educator. One of the most amazing (and frustrating) things about being an educator is that there is always room for improvement. As educators, we get to inspire and impact students every day. We get to explore the "weather" in our classrooms and determine if school is a positive experience or an anxiety-ridden experience for the young people we serve.

Becoming a No-Nonsense Nurturer is not a destination; it is a journey! How you work on the art and science of your chosen craft determines your success and the success of generations of students. Please ensure you are providing a supportive, safe, joy-filled classroom culture—it is imperative to allow for high-quality, rigorous learning to happen in your classroom every day.

Why do the steps and strategies of the No-Nonsense Nurturer four-step model work so well for *all* educators and *all* students? The answer is simple: the four-step model is based on what high-performing teachers with proven practice do to support their students. Codifying and explicitly unpacking what the best of the best do in their classrooms will help you create a culture in your own classroom to serve *every student, every day.*

Precise directions are the starting point for setting up yourself and your students for success. When planning your precise directions, challenge yourself to reflect on what you want the learning objective to look like and feel like for your students. By planning and reflecting on your directions, you not only build relationships with students by demonstrating your care for them but also demonstrate that, with some planning and attention to detail, success is always within your students' grasp.

Positive narration brings joy to your classroom. While it isn't praise, it makes everyone feel good when you notice the positive. The narrated student enjoys hearing his or her name associated with what he or she is doing right. For those who need extra support, hearing narration gives him or her the opportunity to see what he or she needs to be doing to engage. As the teacher, narration reminds you that many of your students are on task, engaged, and excited about learning in your classroom. Positivity breeds positive momentum, which is essential for a joyful classroom culture.

Accountability systems provide logical consequences, the opportunity for life lessons, and the chance to build relationships not just between teacher and student but also among students as they strive to reach common behavioral and academic goals. Teaching students accountability and self-discipline helps them to be successful during their school careers but also in life. Incentive systems that build collective efficacy support both teacher-student and student-student relationships, increasing the positive culture and supports for all stakeholders in a No-Nonsense Nurturer's classroom.

Relationships are the cornerstone for human beings. We thrive with positive human interactions. We feel validated when we find commonalities among one another and humanized when others acknowledge our values and cultures. Our students can be our greatest teachers, as they are masters of their communities and cultures. By learning with and through them, we become better teachers and, ultimately, better human beings.

While the four-step model might feel like a program at first, being a No-Nonsense Nurturer is actually an education philosophy. How you view students and their families and the impact you can have on future generations is what drives the values, beliefs, and mindsets of your classroom. This can impact students well beyond their academic careers.

Understanding young people and supporting their development and success are the most important jobs in the world. Thank you for allowing this work to be part of your journey.

Video

This brief video montage was designed for readers to view the steps of the No-Nonsense Nurturer four-step model individually and in teams. Scan this code to view No-Nonsense Nurturers as they demonstrate the No-Nonsense Nurturer four-step model in action.

**No-Nonsense Nurturer Four-Step
Model in Action**

www.ct3education.com/book/four-step-model

Reflection Activities

The reflection activities on page 188–189 are designed to help you reflect on your current professional practice and support your journey to becoming a No-Nonsense Nurturer. You may choose to complete them individually or in teams.

Record Your Thoughts

Take a minute to answer the following questions and complete the No-Nonsense Nurturer ideas four-square.

• What concepts do I want to bring into my classroom every day? • What are some concepts I am not yet comfortable with that I want to discuss with a colleague or trusted friend? • What are the concepts I am currently implementing or will implement tomorrow? • What are some things I need to plan for? Keep the four-square in a place that is visible so you keep moving forward as a No-Nonsense Nurturer.	
Wow! These ideas make sense to me!	Hmm . . . These ideas are bit controversial.
Wow! I can implement these ideas right away!	Hmm . . . I need to think more about how to implement these ideas and concepts.

Reflect and Journal

Now that you have reached the end of this book, take some time to reflect on everything you've learned about becoming a No-Nonsense Nurturer and how you can implement some of the strategies and tools in your classroom.

Part 1

What type of teacher will you choose to be every day? Take thirty minutes and reflect on the type of teacher you want to be. How will you set up your students for success? How will you build meaningful relationships with each of them, especially the ones you find most challenging? How will you ensure you are satisfied with your career choice? What do you want students to say about you when they reflect back on school ten years from now?

_____

Part 2

This is one of my favorite (slightly altered) quotes by Johann Wolfgang von Goethe (n.d.). How can you use this quote to inspire yourself in your journey as a No-Nonsense Nurturer?

> *I have come to a frightening conclusion. I am the decisive element in the classroom. It is my personal approach that creates the climate. It is my daily mood that makes the weather. As a teacher, I possess tremendous power to make a child's life miserable or joyous. I can be a tool of torture or an instrument of inspiration. I can humiliate or humor, hurt or heal. In all situations, it is my response that decides whether a crisis will be escalated or de-escalated, and a person is humanized or de-humanized.*

_____

Source: Von Goethe, J. W., n.d.

REFERENCES & RESOURCES

Addy, S., & Wight, V. R. (2012). *Basic facts about low-income children, 2010: Children under age 18.* New York: National Center for Children in Poverty.

Adkins-Coleman, T. A. (2010). "I'm not afraid to come into your world": Case studies of teachers facilitating engagement in urban high school English classrooms. *The Journal of Negro Education, 79*(1), 41–53.

Aloe, A. M., Amo, L. C., & Shanahan, M. E. (2014). Classroom management self-efficacy and burnout: A multivariate meta-analysis. *Educational Psychology Review, 26*(1), 101–126.

Asch, C. M. (2010). The inadvertent bigotry of inappropriate expectations. *Education Week, 29*(35), 35.

Baldwin, S. C., Buchanan, A. M., & Rudisill, M. D. (2007). What teacher candidates learned about diversity, social justice, and themselves from service-learning experiences. *Journal of Teacher Education, 58*(4), 315–327.

Berry, B., Hopkins-Thompson, P., & Hoke, M. (2002). *Assessing and supporting new teachers: Lessons from the southeast—Teaching quality in the southeast policy brief.* Chapel Hill, NC: Southeast Center for Teaching Quality.

Bill & Melinda Gates Foundation. (2010). *Learning about teaching: Initial findings from the Measures of Effective Teaching project.* Accessed at www.metproject.org /downloads/Preliminary_Finding-Policy_Brief.pdf on April 16, 2018.

Bloom, B. S. (Ed.). (1956). *Taxonomy of educational objectives: The classification of educational goals; Handbook I: Cognitive domain.* New York: McKay.

Bondy, E., & Ross, D. D. (2008). The teacher as warm demander. *Educational Leadership, 66*(1), 54–58.

Bondy, E., Ross, D. D., Gallingane, C., & Hambacher, E. (2007). Creating environments of success and resilience: Culturally responsive classroom management and more. *Urban Education, 42*(4), 326–348.

Bondy, E., Ross, D. D., Hambacher, E., & Acosta, M. (2013). Becoming warm demanders: Perspectives and practices of first year teachers. *Urban Education, 48*(3), 420–450.

Borrero, N. (2011). Entering teaching for and with love: Visions of pre-service urban teachers. *Journal of Urban Learning, Teaching, and Research, 7,* 18–26.

Bradley, R. H., Corwyn, R. F., Burchinal, M., McAdoo, H. P., & Coll, C. G. (2001). The home environments of children in the United States, part 1: Variations by age, ethnicity, and poverty status. *Child Development, 72*(6), 1844–1867.

Brooks-Gunn, J., & Markman, L. B. (2005). The contribution of parenting to ethnic and racial gaps in school readiness. *The Future of Children, 15*(1), 139–168.

Brotman, L. M., Calzada, E., Huang, K., Kingston, S., Dawson-McClure, S., Kamboukos, D., . . . Petkova, E. (2011). Promoting effective parenting practices and preventing child behavior problems in school among ethnically diverse families from underserved, urban communities. *Child Development, 82*(1), 258–276.

Brown, D. F. (2004). Urban teachers' professed classroom management strategies: Reflections of culturally responsive teaching. *Urban Education, 39*(3), 266–289.

Camangian, P. (2010). Starting with self: Teaching autoethnography to foster critically caring literacies. *Research in the Teaching of English, 45*(2), 179–204.

Canter, L. (2010). *Assertive discipline: Positive behavior management for today's classroom* (4th ed.). Bloomington, IN: Solution Tree Press.

Canter, L. (2014). *Lee Canter's classroom management for academic success.* Bloomington, IN: Solution Tree Press.

Canter, L., & Canter, M. (1976). *Assertive discipline: A take charge approach for today's educator.* Seal Beach, CA: Author.

Chang, M.-L. (2009). An appraisal perspective of teacher burnout: Examining the emotional work of teachers. *Educational Psychology Review, 21*(3), 193–218.

Charles, C. M. (1999). *Building classroom discipline* (6th ed.). New York: Longman.

Compton-Lilly, C. (2003). *Reading families: The literate lives of urban children*. New York: Teachers College Press.

Consequence. (n.d.). In *Merriam-Webster online*. Accessed at https://merriam-webster.com/dictionary/consequences on April 13, 2018.

Cotton, K., & Wikelund, K. (1990). *Educational time factors*. Portland, OR: Northwest Regional Educational Laboratory.

Delpit, L. D. (2006). *Other people's children: Cultural conflict in the classroom*. New York: New Press.

Delpit, L. D. (2012). *"Multiplication is for white people": Raising expectations for other people's children*. New York: New Press.

Deschenes, S., Cuban, L., & Tyack, D. (2001). Mismatch: Historical perspectives on schools and students who don't fit them. *Teachers College Record, 103*(4), 525–547.

Dicke, T., Parker, P. D., Marsh, H. W., Kunter, M., Schmeck, A., & Leutner, D. (2014). Self-efficacy in classroom management, classroom disturbances, and emotional exhaustion: A moderated mediation analysis of teacher candidates. *Journal of Educational Psychology, 106*(2), 569.

Duncan-Andrade, J. (2007). Gangstas, wankstas, and ridas: Defining, developing and supporting effective teachers in urban schools. *International Journal of Quantitative Studies in Education, 20*(6), 617–638.

Dweck, C. S. (2007). The perils and promises of praise. *Educational Leadership, 65*(2), 34–39.

Eccles, J. S., & Harold, R. D. (1993). Parent-school involvement during the early adolescent years. *Teachers College Record, 94*(3), 568–587.

Emdin, C. (2016). *For white folks who teach in the hood . . . and the rest of y'all too: Reality pedagogy in urban education*. Boston: Beacon Press.

Erdogan, M., Kursun, E., Sisman, G. T., Saltan, F., Gok, A., & Yildiz, I. (2010). A qualitative study on classroom management and classroom discipline problems, reasons, and solutions: A case of information technologies class. *Educational Sciences: Theory and Practice, 10*(2), 881–891.

Excerpts from Bush's speech on improving education. (1999, September 3). *The New York Times*. Accessed at www.nytimes.com/1999/09/03/us/excerpts-from-bush-s-speech-on-improving-education.html on July 26, 2018.

Farkas, S., Johnson, J., Duffett, A., & Foleno, T. (2001). *Trying to stay ahead of the game: Superintendents and principals talk about school leadership.* New York: Public Agenda.

Farr, S. (2010). *Teaching as leadership: The highly effective teacher's guide to closing the achievement gap.* San Francisco: Jossey-Bass.

Ferguson, M. (2013). Praise: What does the literature say? What are the implications for teachers? *Kairaranga, 14*(2), 35–39.

Ferguson, R. F. (2008). Helping students of color meet high standards. In M. Pollock (Ed.), *Everyday antiracism: Getting real about race in school* (pp. 78–81). New York: New Press.

Fisher, D., & Frey, N. (2013). *Better learning through structured teaching: A framework for the gradual release of responsibility.* Alexandria, VA: The Association for Supervision and Curriculum Development.

Fram, M. S. (2003). *Managing to parent: Social support, social capital, and parenting practices among welfare-participating mothers with young children.* Institute for Research on Poverty Discussion Paper No. 1263-03. Madison, WI: University of Wisconsin.

Freedman, S. W., & Appleman, D. (2009). "In it for the long haul": How teacher education can contribute to teacher retention in high-poverty, urban schools. *Journal of Teacher Education, 60*(3), 323–337.

Freire, P. (1970). *Pedagogy of the oppressed.* New York: Herder and Herder.

Gibbs, N. (2005). Parents behaving badly. *Time, 165*(8), 40–49.

Greenberg, J., Putman, H., & Walsh, K. (2014). *Training our future teachers: Classroom management* (Rev.). Washington, DC: National Council on Teacher Quality.

Gregory, A., Clawson, K., Davis, A., & Gerewitz, J. (2014). The promise of restorative practices to transform teacher-student relationships and achieve equity in school discipline. *Journal of Educational and Psychological Consultation, 26*(4), 325–353.

Haberman, M. (2004a). *Star teachers: The ideology and best practice of effective teachers of diverse children and youth in poverty.* Houston, TX: Haberman Educational Foundation.

Haberman, M. (2004b). *Teacher burnout in black and white.* Houston, TX: Haberman Educational Foundation.

Hammond, Z. (2015). *Culturally responsive teaching and the brain: Promoting authentic engagement and rigor among culturally and linguistically diverse students.* Thousand Oaks, CA: Corwin Press.

Hattie, J. (2012). *Visible learning for teachers: Maximizing impact on learning.* New York: Routledge.

Hattie, J. (2016). *The current status of the visible learning research.* Third Annual Visible Learning Conference: Mindframes and Maximizers. Washington, DC, July 11, 2016.

Henderson, A. T., & Mapp, K. L. (2002). *A new wave of evidence: The impact of school, family, and community connections on student achievement.* Austin, TX: Southwest Educational Development Laboratory.

Hill, N. E., & Torres, K. (2010). Negotiating the American dream: The paradox of aspirations and achievement among Latino students and engagement between their families and schools. *Journal of Social Issues, 66*(1), 95–112.

Howard, G. R. (1999). *We can't teach what we don't know: White teachers, multiracial schools.* New York: Teachers College Press.

Hudson, P. (2012). How can schools support beginning teachers? A call for timely induction and mentoring for effective teaching. *Australian Journal of Teacher Education, 37*(7), 70–84.

Irvine, J. J. (2003). *Educating teachers for diversity: Seeing with a cultural eye.* New York: Teachers College Press.

Irvine, J. J., & Fraser, J. W. (1998). Warm demanders. *Education Week, 17*(35), 56.

Jensen, E. (2009). *Teaching with poverty in mind: What being poor does to kids' brains and what schools can do about it.* Alexandria, VA: Association for Supervision and Curriculum Development.

Jiang, Y., Ekono, M., & Skinner, C. (2015). *Basic facts about low-income children: Children under 18 years, 2013.* New York: National Center for Children in Poverty.

Jones, F. (2000). *Tools for teaching.* Santa Cruz, CA: Author.

Jussim, L., & Harber, K. D. (2005). Teacher expectations and self-fulfilling prophecies: Knowns and unknowns, resolved and unresolved controversies. *Personality and Social Psychology Review, 9*(2), 131–155.

Kafele, B. K. (2013). *Closing the attitude gap: How to fire up your students to strive for success.* Alexandria, VA: Association for Supervision and Curriculum Development.

Klei Borrero, K., & Canter, L. (2018). *No-nonsense nurturer* (Version 2.2) [Online course]. Accessed at www.ct3education.com/online-learning on July 26, 2018.

Kohl, H. (1994). *"I won't learn from you," and other thoughts on creative maladjustment.* New York: New Press.

Kopp, W. (2011). *A chance to make history: What works and what doesn't in providing an excellent education for all.* New York: Public Affairs.

Kounin, J. S. (1970). *Discipline and group management in classrooms.* New York: Holt, Rinehart and Winston.

Kumar, R., & Hamer, L. (2013). Preservice teachers' attitudes and beliefs toward student diversity and proposed instructional practices: A sequential design study. *Journal of Teacher Education, 64*(2), 162–177.

Ladd, H. F., & Fiske, E. B. (2011, December 11). Class matters. Why won't we admit it? *New York Times*, A23.

Ladson-Billings, G. (1994). *The dreamkeepers: Successful teachers of African American children.* San Francisco: Jossey-Bass.

Langdon, C. (1996). The third Phi Delta Kappa poll of teachers' attitudes toward the public schools. *Phi Delta Kappan, 78*(3), 244–250.

Lareau, A., & Horvat, E. M. (1999). Moments of social inclusion and exclusion: Race, class, and cultural capital in family-school relationships. *Sociology of education*, 37–53.

Lemov, D. (2010). *Teach like a champion: 49 techniques that put students on the path to college.* San Francisco: Jossey-Bass.

Lemov, D. (2015). *Teach like a champion 2.0: 62 techniques that put students on the path to college* (2nd ed.). San Francisco: Jossey-Bass.

Libbey, H. P. (2004). Measuring student relationships to school: Attachment, bonding, connectedness, and engagement. *The Journal of School Health, 74*(7), 274–283.

Lombardi, V. (n.d.). *BrainyQuote*. Accessed at https://brainyquote.com/quotes /vince_lombardi_138158 on June 6, 2018.

Losen, D. J., & Skiba, R. J. (2010). *Suspended education: Urban middle schools in crisis*. Montgomery, AL: Southern Poverty Law Center.

Marzano, R. J. (2003). *Classroom management that works: Research-based strategies for every teacher*. Alexandria, VA: Association for Supervision and Curriculum Development.

Marzano, R. J. (2010). Art and science of teaching: High expectations for all. *Educational Leadership, 68*(1), 82–84.

Marzano, R. J., & Marzano, J. S. (2003). The key to classroom management. *Educational Leadership, 61*(1), 6–13.

McAllister, G., & Irvine, J. J. (2002). The role of empathy in teaching culturally diverse students: A qualitative study of teachers' beliefs. *Journal of Teacher Education, 53*(5), 433–443.

Milner, H. R. (2006). Classroom management in urban classrooms. In C. M. Evertson & C. S. Weinstein (Eds.), *Handbook of classroom management: Research, practice, and contemporary issues* (pp. 491–522). Mahwah, NJ: Erlbaum.

Milner IV, H. R. (2007). African American males in urban schools: No excuses— teach and empower. *Theory Into Practice, 46*(3), 239–246.

Mixon, K. (2012, May 2). *Classroom management that creates harmony instead of hostility*. Accessed at www.edweek.org/tm/articles/2012/05/02/fp_mixen _classroommanagement.html on September 11, 2018

Monroe, C. R., & Obidah, J. E. (2004). The influence of cultural synchronization on a teacher's perceptions of disruption: A case study of an African American middle-school classroom. *Journal of Teacher Education, 55*(3), 256–268.

Mouton, S. G., Hawkins, J., McPherson, R. H., & Copley, J. (1996). School attachment: Perspectives of low-attached high school students. *Educational Psychology, 16*(3), 297–304.

National Center on Safe and Supportive Learning Environments. (2018). *School climate*. Accessed at https://safesupportivelearning.ed.gov/safe-and-healthy -students/school-climate on July 27, 2018.

National Research Council. (2004). *Engaging schools: Fostering high school students' motivation to learn*. Washington, DC: The National Academies Press.

Nieto, S. (2002). *Language, culture, and teaching: Critical perspectives for a new century.* Mahwah, NJ: Erlbaum.

Nieto, S. (2008). Nice is not enough: Defining caring for students of color. In M. Pollock (Ed.)., *Everyday antiracism: Getting real about race in school* (pp. 28–31). New York: New Press.

Noguera, P. (2003). *City schools and the American dream: Reclaiming the promise of public education.* New York: Teachers College Press.

Obidah, J. E., & Teel, K. M. (2001). *Because of the kids: Facing racial and cultural differences in schools.* New York: Teachers College Press.

Oliver, R. M., & Reschly, D. J. (2007). *Effective classroom management: Teacher preparation and professional development.* Washington, DC: National Comprehensive Center for Teacher Quality.

Paris, D., & Alim, S. (2014). Culturally sustaining pedagogy: A needed change in stance, terminology, and practice. *Harvard Educational Review, 84*(1), 93–97.

Patrick, H., Turner, J., Meyer, D. K, & Midgley, C. (2004). How teachers establish psychological environments during the first days of school: Associations with avoidance in mathematics. *Teachers College Record, 105*(8), 1521–1558.

Peske, H. G., & Haycock, K. (2006). *Teaching inequality: How poor and minority students are shortchanged on teacher quality.* Washington, DC: The Education Trust.

Picower, B. (2012). Using their words: Six elements of social justice curriculum design for the elementary classroom. *International Journal of Multicultural Education, 14*(1), 1–17.

Pope, D. (2001). *Doing school: How we are creating a generation of stressed out, materialistic, and miseducated students.* New Haven, CT: Yale University Press.

Public Agenda. (2004). *Teaching interrupted: Do discipline policies in today's public schools foster the common good?* New York: Public Agenda.

Punishment. (n.d.). In *Merriam-Webster online.* Accessed at https://merriam-webster .com/dictionary/punishment on April 16, 2018.

Responsive Classroom. (2011, September 2). *Punishment vs. logical consequences.* Accessed at www.responsiveclassroom.org/punishment-vs-logical-consequences on September 12, 2018.

Rist, R. (1970). Student social class and teacher expectations: The self-fulfilling prophecy in ghetto education. *Harvard Educational Review, 40*(3), 411–451.

Rosenthal, R., & Jacobson, L. (1968). Pygmalion in the classroom. *The Urban Review, 3*(1), 16–20.

Ross, D. D., Bondy, E., Gallingane, C., & Hambacher, E. (2008). Promoting academic engagement through insistence: Being a warm demander. *Childhood Education, 84*(3), 142–146.

Rothstein-Fisch, C., & Trumbull, E. (2008). *Managing diverse classrooms: How to build on students' cultural strengths.* Alexandria, VA: Association for Supervision and Curriculum Development.

Rushton, S. P. (2003). Two preservice teachers' growth in self-efficacy while teaching in an inner-city school. *Urban Review, 35*(3), 167–189.

Sealey-Ruiz, Y., & Greene, P. (2015). Popular visual images and the (mis)reading of black male youth: A case for racial literacy in urban preservice teacher education. *Teaching Education, 26*(1), 55–76.

Shevalier, R., & McKenzie, B. A. (2012). Culturally responsive teaching as an ethics- and care-based approach to urban education. *Urban Education, 47*(6), 1086–1105.

Shumate, E. D., & Wills, H. P. (2010). Classroom-based functional analysis and intervention for disruptive and off-task behaviors. *Education and Treatment of Children, 33*(1), 23–48.

Siwatu, K. O. (2011). Preservice teachers' sense of preparedness and self-efficacy to teach in America's urban and suburban schools: Does context matter? *Teaching and Teacher Education, 27*(2), 357–365.

Steele, C. (2004). A threat in the air. In J. Banks & C. Banks (Eds.), *Handbook of Research on Multicultural Education* (pp. 682–698). San Francisco: Jossey-Bass.

Stefanakis, E. H. (2000). Teachers' judgments do count: Assessing bilingual students. In Z. F. Beykont (Ed.), *Lifting Every Voice* (pp. 139–160). Cambridge, MA: Harvard Education Publishing Group.

Tenenbaum, H. R., & Ruck, M. D. (2007). Are teachers' expectations different for racial minority than for European American students? A meta-analysis. *Journal of Educational Psychology, 99*(2), 253.

Thompson, G. L. (2004). *Through ebony eyes: What teachers need to know but are afraid ask about African-American students.* San Francisco: Jossey-Bass.

Trumbull, E., Diaz-Meza, R., Hasan, A., & Rothstein-Fisch, C. (2001). *The bridging cultures project five-year report: 1996–2000.* San Francisco: WestEd.

U.S. Department of Education. (2016). *The state of racial diversity in the educator workforce.* Washington, DC: Author. Accessed at https://ed.gov/rschstat/eval /highered/racial-diversity/state-racial-diversity-workforce.pdf on April 16, 2018.

Vaden-Kiernan, N., McManus, J., & Chapman, C. (2005). *Parent and family involvement in education: 2002–03 (NCES 2005–043).* U.S. Department of Education, National Center for Education Statistics. Washington, DC: U.S. Government Printing Office.

Valenzuela, A. (1999). *Subtractive schooling: U.S.-Mexican youth and the politics of caring.* Albany, NY: State University of New York Press.

von Goethe, J. W. (n.d.). *Essential life skills: Inspiring Johann Wolfgang Von Goethe quotes.* Accessed at www.essentiallifeskills.net/inspiring-goethe-quotes.html on August 6, 2018.

Vygotsky, L. S. (1978). *Mind in society: The development of higher psychological processes.* Cambridge, MA: Harvard University Press.

Walker, C., Colvin, G., & Ramsey, E. (1995). *Antisocial behavior in school: Strategies and best practices.* Belmont, CA: Thomson Brooks/Cole Publishing.

Walker-Dalhouse, D. (2005). Discipline: Responding to socioeconomic and racial differences. *Childhood Education, 82*(1), 24–30.

Ware, F. (2006). Warm demander pedagogy: Culturally responsive teaching that supports a culture of achievement for African American students. *Urban Education, 41*(4), 427–456.

Weiner, L. (1999). *Urban teaching: The essentials.* New York: Teachers College Press.

Weinstein, C. S. (1998). "I want to be nice, but I have to be mean": Exploring prospective teachers' conceptions of caring and order. *Teaching and Teacher Education, 14*(2), 153–163.

Weinstein, C. S., & Mignano, A. J., Jr. (2003). *Elementary classroom management: Lessons from research and practice* (3rd ed.). Boston: McGraw-Hill.

Weinstein, C. S., Tomlinson-Clarke, S., & Curran, M. (2004). Toward a conception of culturally responsive classroom management. *Journal of Teacher Education, 55*(1), 25–38.

Wentzel, K. R. (2003). Motivating students to behave in socially competent ways. *Theory Into Practice, 42*(4), 319–326.

Wilson, B. L., & Corbett, H. D. (2001). *Listening to urban kids: School reform and the teachers they want.* Albany, NY: State University of New York Press.

Yang, K. W. (2009). Discipline or punish? Some suggestions for school policy and teacher practice. *Language Arts, 87*(1), 49–61.

Yosso, T. J. (2005). Whose culture has capital? A critical race theory discussion of community cultural wealth. *Race, Ethnicity, and Education, 8*(1), 69–91.

INDEX